Generative AI for Beginners: A Complete Introduction

Aeronis Krynn

Let me guess—you've been hearing the buzz. Generative AI. Deepfakes. ChatGPT. That robot that can write poetry better than your cousin Kyle. And now you're here, cracking open this book, wondering what kind of sorcery is happening behind the curtain. Well, welcome. You've just stepped into the neon-lit, slightly chaotic, endlessly fascinating world of Generative AI.

I'm Aeronis Krynn, your guide-slash-nerd-in-residence for this ride. If this is your first dip into artificial intelligence, don't worry. I'm not here to drown you in math or drop you in some PhD-level rabbit hole where every other sentence includes Greek letters and mysterious matrix operations. Nope. This book—**Generative AI for Beginners: A Complete Introduction**—is the friendlier, slightly caffeinated tour bus through the wild frontier of machines that can create.

Yes, create. Not just compute, not just sort spreadsheets, but write, draw, sing, compose, dream. These models are the artists of the AI family, and they're here to show us what happens when you mix math with imagination. Which, it turns out, is a lot cooler than it sounds.

Now, here's the secret sauce: this book is part of a larger saga, a full-on quest if you will. I call it *The Generative AI Blueprint*—a series of ten books that are basically your treasure map to becoming a certified AI wizard. If this book is your cozy tavern where you gather your supplies and meet your quirky mentor (hi, that's me), then the others are your armor, your spellbooks, and your dragon-slaying gear.

Here's the lineup of your future adventures:

Generative AI for Beginners: A Complete Introduction (the one you're holding, good choice)

Python for AI: Build Generative Models from Scratch (because even the best sorcerers need to code)

Deep Learning Essentials: Master Neural Networks for AI (welcome to brain-building boot camp)

Autoencoders & VAEs: Hands-On Generative AI Projects (for when you're ready to play with cool toys)

GANs in Action: Create Realistic Images & Videos with AI (where your AI starts painting like Van Gogh with better lighting)

Transformers & GPT: Build and Fine-Tune Large Language Models (yes, the bots that can write novels and flirt better than you)

Stable Diffusion & AI Art: Generate Stunning Images with AI (pure visual magic, no Photoshop required)

Multimodal AI: How to Combine Text, Images & Video with AI (Frankenstein-ing your models, in the best way)

Fine-Tuning & Deploying AI Models: A Practical Guide (shipping your AI creation into the world—no bubble wrap needed)

The Future of Generative AI: Ethics, Careers & Business Applications (aka: "how to be a good AI sorcerer and not accidentally summon Skynet")

But let's not get ahead of ourselves. This first book is the tavern, remember? And before you start sword-fighting with neural networks, we need to get you properly briefed.

We're going to start from the very beginning—what even is artificial intelligence? I'll tell you where it came from, how it's evolved, and why it's finally having its Hollywood moment. Then we'll dig into machine learning (the slightly nerdy cousin of AI), and peel back the layers until we reach the creamy center: Generative AI.

This isn't just AI that answers questions or plays chess. This is the kind that dreams. It predicts pixels. It finishes your sentences—sometimes creepily well. It mimics voices, composes music, and yes, writes intros for books like this one. In fact, if I suddenly start sounding more eloquent halfway through this paragraph, there's a non-zero chance a language model hijacked my keyboard.

But don't panic. You're still early. And that's a good thing.

The world is only just waking up to what generative models can do. Businesses are scrambling to hire people who understand this stuff. Artists are wrestling with what it means for creativity. Students are wondering if their homework will be written by robots (short answer: possibly). And in the middle of it all, here you are—deciding to learn how this magic trick works.

And here's the thing: you can learn this. Seriously. If you can understand Netflix recommendations and why your phone autocorrects "ducking," you can understand generative AI. You don't need a computer science degree. You don't need to be a math genius. You need curiosity, a willingness to play, and the ability to laugh when your AI model tries to draw a cat and ends up with a toaster.

Each chapter of this book is a step deeper into the rabbit hole. We'll start with the foundations of AI and machine learning, then gently transition into what makes generative models so different. I'll introduce you to the cast of characters—autoencoders, GANs, transformers, diffusion models. They each have their quirks, like that one friend who insists on only speaking in Shakespearean sonnets. But once you get to know them, you'll see how insanely powerful they are.

By the time we're done, you'll have hands-on experience. You'll run real models. You'll generate text and images. You'll mess up (we all do), and then you'll get better. And if the spark catches—if you finish this book and think, "Hey, I want to go deeper"—well, good news. That's why I wrote the rest of The Generative AI Blueprint. Consider this your launchpad.

Now, before we jump into Chapter 1, a quick warning. This stuff is addictive. The first time your code spits out a brand new sentence or image, made from nothing but numbers and noise? That's the moment. You'll be hooked. And then, like me, you'll be up at 2 a.m. feeding prompts into a chatbot to see if it can write poetry in pirate-speak (yes, it can).

So buckle up. Stretch your fingers. Fire up your imagination. Because this is where it all begins.

Let's go make some AI magic.

Chapter 1: Understanding Artificial Intelligence

Let me paint you a picture: You're sipping coffee, scrolling your feed, and you see a talking toaster arguing politics with a blender. That's not the future—it's Tuesday in the age of AI. But before we get into the wild world of machines that talk, draw, write, and maybe even judge your Spotify playlists, let's roll it back. What even is artificial intelligence? And why is everyone from Elon Musk to your grandma suddenly obsessed with it?

This chapter lays the foundation for your journey into AI. We'll define artificial intelligence in its broadest sense, explore its fascinating history from mid-century dream to mainstream disruptor, and draw important distinctions between narrow and general AI. You'll also get an essential overview of how machine learning and deep learning fit into the picture, and why generative AI is the star of today's AI renaissance.

1.1 What is Artificial Intelligence?

Let's start with the big one. The question everyone asks at parties the moment they find out I work in AI. Right after, "So… should we be worried?" and just before, "Can I make an AI that does my taxes?"

First, let me clarify: AI doesn't currently want to conquer the world, fall in love, or write Shakespeare (although it can, badly). But the idea of Artificial Intelligence is way older and way weirder than most people think—and way less like Hollywood portrays it. If you're picturing sentient robots with glowing red eyes, slow that sci-fi roll. We're not there. Yet.

So what is artificial intelligence?

In the most no-nonsense terms: Artificial Intelligence is the field of computer science focused on creating machines that can perform tasks that typically require human intelligence. That's it. Nothing mystical, nothing evil—just machines trying to do smart things.

These tasks can range from super simple (like identifying a cat in a photo) to brain-bendingly complex (like generating a realistic fake photo of a cat playing the guitar in a Renaissance painting). Some AIs can diagnose diseases, compose music, chat like a sarcastic friend, or beat grandmasters at chess and Go. Others just recommend what you should watch next on Netflix. (Thanks, AI. I didn't need to sleep anyway.)

A Brief Detour: Why We Call It "Artificial"

"Artificial" doesn't mean "fake." It means "man-made." Think of artificial sweeteners—sure, they're not sugar, but they still mess with your coffee. In the same way, artificial intelligence isn't human intelligence, but it can simulate certain behaviors of it. Sometimes convincingly, sometimes hilariously not.

At its core, AI is just a big math-and-code engine trained to make predictions, decisions, or outputs based on data. Think of it like teaching a dog tricks, but instead of using treats, you're using thousands (or millions) of labeled examples. The AI doesn't "understand" the world—it just learns patterns and mimics them. Like an overenthusiastic intern that works really fast and doesn't ask for coffee breaks.

The Three Flavors of AI (So Far)

Let me quickly give you the lay of the land. AI generally falls into three rough categories:

Narrow AI (Weak AI) – This is the AI we have today. It's built to do one thing really well. Like facial recognition, voice assistants, or spam filtering. Siri can tell you a joke, but she won't suddenly invent quantum teleportation. She's clever, not conscious.

General AI (Strong AI) – This is the theoretical holy grail. A machine with the general reasoning and learning capacity of a human. It can transfer knowledge from one domain to another, solve new problems on the fly, and maybe even outwit your teenager. We're not there yet, and honestly, some of us hope we never get there without serious safeguards.

Superintelligence – This one's mostly sci-fi. It's the level beyond humans—machines that can improve themselves and outthink us in every field. Think HAL 9000, Ultron, or that one weird AI in every dystopian novel that says "I am doing this for your own good."

Right now, we're solidly in Narrow AI territory. Which, let's be honest, is more than enough to keep us entertained, amazed, and occasionally terrified.

So… How Does It Actually Work?

Let me break it down like I'm explaining it to my skeptical uncle at Thanksgiving.

Most modern AI is powered by a branch called machine learning (ML). That's where we don't program the machine with a bunch of rules. Instead, we show it data and let it learn the rules on its own. Kind of like how toddlers learn not to stick forks in electrical sockets—except with less crying and fewer lawsuits.

Within machine learning, there are even fancier layers like deep learning, where we use neural networks (inspired very loosely by the human brain) to find patterns in massive oceans of data. The bigger and deeper the network, the more complex the patterns it can recognize.

But—and this is important—AI still doesn't "think." It doesn't know what a cat is. It's just gotten really, really good at spotting pixel patterns that look like cats based on statistical correlations. It's glorified curve-fitting, not consciousness.

The Many Faces of Intelligence

The phrase "artificial intelligence" covers a surprisingly wide spectrum of skills. Some AIs are built for vision (like self-driving cars spotting pedestrians), others for language (like the one you're reading right now), and still others for creativity (like AI-generated art or music).

These systems don't share one giant brain—they're individually trained for specific purposes. Which is why your email filter can stop spam, but can't write a rap battle between Shakespeare and Elon Musk. (Actually, some can. Welcome to Generative AI.)

The "Wow" and the "Whoa There" Moments

AI gives us moments of pure magic—like watching an AI generate a painting in the style of Van Gogh or translate live speech across languages in real time. But it also raises a bunch of ethical eyebrows: bias in data, deepfakes, surveillance, and who's ultimately responsible when things go wrong.

The power of AI is growing fast. Like, "hold-onto-your-sandwich" fast. That's why it's more important than ever for regular people—not just tech bros in hoodies—to understand what AI is, what it can (and can't) do, and how to use it responsibly.

Spoiler: You don't have to be a PhD-wielding data wizard to get this stuff. You just need a curious brain and maybe a decent internet connection. (And hey, you've got at least one of those. Good start.)

So… Is It Really "Intelligent"?

Here's the spicy take: No. Not really. Not yet.

AI doesn't understand the world. It doesn't feel, doesn't have goals, doesn't dream of electric sheep. It just processes input and spits out output based on training. But because it's really good at faking it, it can feel intelligent to us. That's why people name their chatbots or feel weirdly emotional when their AI art generator makes something beautiful.

It's less about true intelligence and more about impressive imitation. Kind of like a parrot that can quote Shakespeare—it's not writing sonnets, but it sounds cool anyway.

And that's the lowdown on what artificial intelligence really is. If you walked in thinking AI was magic, I hope you now see it as what it truly is: powerful, mathematical, misunderstood—and kind of like your weird cousin who's super smart but can't explain anything without a diagram.

Next up, we'll hop into the history of AI—how it went from philosophers' daydreams to algorithms that now write clickbait articles and finish your sentences. Spoiler: It's a wild ride.

Hold onto your neural nets—we're just getting started.

1.2 History and Evolution of AI

If you think AI suddenly showed up one day like a tech bro with a new startup idea, think again. The dream of artificial intelligence has been around for literally thousands of years. (And spoiler: the ancient Greeks didn't even have Wi-Fi.)

Before we had algorithms and GPUs, we had myths—like Talos, the bronze robot of Crete who protected the island by chucking boulders at invaders. Humanity's been obsessed with the idea of building thinking machines way before TikTok made us question our attention spans.

So how did we get from ancient myths to ChatGPT writing semi-passable poetry? Strap in, friend. It's history time. But don't worry, I'll keep it short, sweet, and almost entirely free of pop quizzes.

The Birth of an Idea (1940s–1950s)

AI as a serious scientific idea didn't really kick off until the mid-20th century, when some very clever humans asked, "Can machines think?" That question came from Alan Turing, who you might know as the godfather of computer science—or that guy Benedict Cumberbatch played in The Imitation Game.

In 1950, Turing published his legendary paper "Computing Machinery and Intelligence", where he proposed the now-famous Turing Test. Simply put: if you can't tell whether you're talking to a machine or a human, the machine wins. (Fun fact: modern chatbots still have a hard time passing it. Sorry, Clippy.)

Fast forward a few years, and in 1956, a bunch of nerdy visionaries got together at a little event called the Dartmouth Conference. They basically invented AI as a field and said, "Yeah, we can totally make machines that think like people... probably by next summer."

Spoiler: it took a bit longer than that.

The Early Hype Train (1950s–1970s)

The early decades were full of optimism, funding, and headlines like "Machines Will Rival Humans Within 20 Years!" Scientists built programs that could solve algebra problems, play simple games, and even prove theorems.

AI was so hyped that governments started shoveling money at it. (Imagine getting paid just to promise you'd build a robot Einstein. Different times.)

Researchers made some impressive demos, but there were… limitations. Like, an AI might be able to solve a chess puzzle but have no clue how to recognize a cat or drive a car. Turns out, "common sense" is really hard to teach a machine.

The AI Winters (1970s–1990s)

Every good story needs some drama—and AI's story has multiple seasons of brutal disappointment called AI winters. Funding dried up, public interest fizzled, and scientists got mocked harder than someone pitching MySpace 2.0 in 2025.

The problem was simple: early AI promised the moon but barely reached the backyard. Computers weren't powerful enough, and the algorithms couldn't scale to real-world problems. People realized building human-like intelligence was a tiny bit more complicated than they thought.

Fun fact: "AI winter" sounds poetic, but to researchers living through it, it felt more like "AI long, freezing, soul-crushing polar vortex."

Machine Learning Steps Up (1990s–2010s)

While everyone was busy being sad, a new approach quietly rose: machine learning. Instead of hard-coding rules for every possible situation (exhausting), why not let computers learn from data?

This was a game-changer.

Machine learning shifted AI from being a glorified if-then-else machine to something that could spot patterns and adapt. In the '90s and 2000s, we saw speech recognition, computer vision, and early recommendation systems get much, much better.

The world didn't notice right away—but the seeds for today's AI boom were being planted.

(Also, around this time, a computer named Deep Blue beat world chess champion Garry Kasparov in 1997. Big deal. I still can't beat my phone at chess, and it taunts me.)

Deep Learning Changes Everything (2010s)

Then came the deep learning revolution—where we built artificial neural networks way deeper and more complex than ever before.

In 2012, a deep learning model crushed a computer vision competition called ImageNet, dramatically outperforming traditional approaches. Suddenly, machines weren't just recognizing blurry cats—they were identifying dog breeds, cancer cells, street signs—you name it.

Tech giants like Google, Facebook, and Microsoft threw billions into AI research. Startups popped up like mushrooms after rain. AI was cool again.

You probably remember when AI started beating world champions at games like Go (thank you, AlphaGo) and generating surreal, slightly terrifying art. Or maybe when Netflix got freakishly good at suggesting what you really wanted to binge.

This wasn't hype anymore. AI was actually delivering.

The Rise of Generative AI (2020s)

Enter: the golden age of Generative AI.

Instead of just recognizing stuff, AI could now create—writing stories, making paintings, composing music, even coding apps.

We got models like GPT-3 (and later GPT-4), Stable Diffusion, DALL-E, and others that could generate text, images, video, and even voice outputs at astonishing quality. Suddenly, AI wasn't just solving problems. It was collaborating. Inspiring. Sometimes creeping us out just a little.

This is the era you're living through right now—and trust me, it's just getting started.

Looking Back (and a Little Ahead)

When you zoom out, the history of AI looks like a roller coaster: thrilling highs, depressing lows, surprise twists, and the occasional existential crisis.

From dusty conference rooms in the 1950s to billion-parameter models in the cloud, AI's journey has been wild. And here's the kicker: we're still very early. Today's systems are powerful, sure, but they're still nowhere near the level of human reasoning, empathy, or creativity (no matter what your AI-generated dating profile says).

The real question isn't "Will AI take over?" It's "How will we shape AI's future?"

And friend, the fact that you're here, reading this, learning about the history—not just the hype—means you're already one step ahead of the curve.

Now dust off those mental circuits, because next up, we're going to tackle one of the biggest debates in AI: Narrow AI vs. General AI. (Spoiler: it's like comparing a Swiss Army knife to a magic wand. Kinda.)

Stay tuned. Stay curious. Stay slightly suspicious of robots offering candy.

1.3 Narrow AI vs General AI

Okay, time for some real talk.

If AI were a superhero, today's AI would be more like Hawkeye (really good at one thing, like archery) than Superman (good at everything, including bad fashion choices).
We throw the word "AI" around a lot, but in reality, there's a huge difference between what most AI can do today and what sci-fi movies promise it can do tomorrow.

Welcome to the eternal cage match: Narrow AI vs General AI. Grab your popcorn.

Narrow AI: The Specialist

Narrow AI, sometimes called Weak AI (no offense), is what we have right now. It's built to do one thing really, really well.

Recognize a cat? Narrow AI.

Predict tomorrow's weather? Narrow AI.

Suggest you buy socks after you bought shoes online? Narrow AI. (Honestly, too good at that one.)

Narrow AIs are like those ultra-specific tools you find in fancy kitchen stores. A banana slicer? A strawberry huller? Yep, extremely effective—but not what you'd call versatile.

These AIs excel within strict boundaries because we train them on very specific tasks. They can analyze massive data sets, spot patterns, make decisions... but only inside their lane.

If you asked an AI trained to recognize cats to suddenly start diagnosing lung cancer, it would short-circuit faster than my brain trying to do taxes.

Examples of Narrow AI:

Siri, Alexa, and Google Assistant (good at voice commands, not so good at life advice)

Spam filters (keeping your inbox clean since 1997)

Recommender systems (Netflix knows you better than your mom now)

Self-driving cars (still learning not to hit random traffic cones)

Key takeaway: Narrow AIs are smart at one thing, stupid at everything else.

General AI: The Holy Grail (But Mostly Science Fiction)

Now imagine a machine that's not just good at one task—but can learn any task a human can.

Write essays. Paint masterpieces. Solve math proofs. Start a business. Give relationship advice (probably better than your roommate).

That's General AI, or Strong AI.

The dream. The legend. The potential existential crisis.

A General AI would have flexible, adaptable intelligence—like us. It could reason, plan, learn new skills without being reprogrammed, and even deal with novel situations it's never encountered before.

Basically, it would be like a digital brain floating around, just waiting for someone to ask it to fix climate change and explain why your plants keep dying.

Examples of General AI:

None. Zip. Nada.

(Unless you count Marvin the Paranoid Android from Hitchhiker's Guide to the Galaxy.)

Key takeaway: General AI doesn't exist yet. But researchers and futurists love to argue (loudly) about when—or if—it will.

Why It Matters

You might be thinking, "Okay, Aeronis, why should I care whether my AI is narrow or general? Just give me the robot butler already."

Here's the thing: understanding this difference keeps your expectations realistic.

Every time you hear someone say "AI is going to take over the world!"...

They're confusing Narrow AI (what we have) with General AI (what we don't).

Narrow AI is transforming industries—medicine, art, transportation, education—you name it.

But it's not conscious. It doesn't "want" anything. It's a super-powered tool, not a mind.

General AI?

That's where all the ethical, philosophical, and sci-fi-grade freakouts start. If we ever achieve it, we're going to need huge new frameworks around trust, safety, rights, and governance.

It's kind of like owning a pet vs. raising a teenager.

Narrow AI is your obedient Labrador. General AI could be your rebellious 17-year-old who just discovered Nietzsche.

So How Close Are We to General AI?

Depends who you ask.

Some researchers say decades.

Some say never.

Some say, "Hey, look over there!" and run away before answering.

Progress is happening, but true, flexible human-like reasoning is incredibly complicated. It's not just about stacking more layers on a neural network. It's about understanding language, emotions, humor, common sense—all the messy, beautiful chaos that makes us human.

Building a machine that "thinks" in that full, nuanced way is like trying to bottle a lightning storm. Possible? Maybe. But we're nowhere near opening that bottle right now without getting seriously electrocuted.

Quick Recap (Because My Coffee Just Kicked In)

Category	Narrow AI	General AI
Scope	One task (or a few related tasks)	Any task a human can do
Current status	Everywhere	Still theoretical
Intelligence	Specialized	Broad and adaptable
Consciousness	Nope	Maybe someday (and that's scary)
Risk of uprising	0%	TBD... keep your robot vacuum on your good side, just in case

Final Thoughts (and a Dash of Humor)

Narrow AI is here, making life more interesting (and occasionally weirder) every day. General AI is still science fiction… but not entirely out of reach.

In the meantime, if your chatbot starts calling you "Master" and asking about overthrowing humanity—unplug it, give yourself a high-five, and maybe call a professional.

Coming up next: we dive into the thrilling rivalry that powers today's AI: Machine Learning vs Deep Learning.

Spoiler: it's like Batman vs Iron Man—tech nerds fighting for world dominance, but with less spandex.

Stay curious, stay caffeinated.

1.4 Machine Learning vs Deep Learning

Let's be real: if you've ever tried Googling "What is Machine Learning vs Deep Learning?", you probably ended up in a rabbit hole of math equations, diagrams, and the creeping realization that you should've just stuck to cat videos.

Good news: I'm here to explain it like a human, not like a textbook written by a caffeinated robot.

And trust me, once you get it, you'll be able to spot the difference faster than you can say "neural network." (Okay, maybe not that fast, but you get the point.)

So, what's the deal? Are Machine Learning and Deep Learning mortal enemies? Besties? Frenemies?

Spoiler: it's a little like the relationship between pizza and deep-dish pizza. One is a category; the other is a bigger, cheesier version inside that category.

Grab a snack. This one's gonna be delicious.

Machine Learning: The Big Umbrella

Machine Learning (ML) is the big idea that showed computers could be more than calculators.

Instead of programming every single rule ("If input A, do output B"), what if we let the computer learn patterns from data?

Imagine you're teaching a kid to recognize bananas.

Traditional programming: "Bananas are yellow, curved, about six inches long, etc." (tons of hard-coded rules)

Machine Learning: Show the kid a thousand pictures of bananas until they figure it out themselves.

Boom. That's ML in a nutshell: computers learn from examples, not explicit instructions.

Some classic types of Machine Learning:

Supervised Learning: You show the model labeled data ("this is a banana, this is a shoe") and it learns.

Unsupervised Learning: No labels. The model finds patterns on its own (kind of like how toddlers discover that everything is sticky).

Reinforcement Learning: Trial and error, with rewards and punishments. Basically, training a digital puppy.

ML is used everywhere: spam detection, stock market predictions, Netflix recommendations (again, why does Netflix know me better than I know myself?).

Deep Learning: The Overachieving Younger Sibling

Now, Deep Learning (DL) is a subset of Machine Learning.

If ML is pizza, DL is a deep-dish, triple-cheese, extra-toppings pizza. Same family, heavier duty.

Deep Learning uses neural networks—algorithms inspired (very loosely) by how human brains work.

But instead of one or two layers of neurons like early models, deep learning networks have dozens, hundreds, even thousands of layers stacked up.

Each layer learns a slightly more complex representation of the data:

First layer: "This is a line."

Next layer: "This is a circle."

Next layer: "This circle has two triangles. It's probably a cat."

Final layer: "Definitely a cat wearing sunglasses."

Deep Learning shines when you have huge amounts of data and lots of computing power.

It powers things like:

Self-driving cars (seeing roads, people, squirrels)

Voice assistants (understanding your weird accents)

Generative AI (like me, hello)

Language translation

Image generation

Without Deep Learning, there's no GPT-4, no DALL-E, no Stable Diffusion. We'd still be back in the dark ages of Clippy and dial-up Internet.

How They Compare (Without the Jargon)

Feature	Machine Learning	Deep Learning
Data requirement	Can work with smaller data sets	Needs massive amounts of data
Hardware	Normal computers often enough	Needs GPUs or TPUs (lots of compute power)
Feature engineering	Humans do a lot of it manually	Model figures out features automatically
Examples	Spam filters, credit scoring	Image recognition, voice assistants, GPT-4

In Machine Learning, humans spend a lot of time picking the right features ("this pixel pattern looks like an ear").

In Deep Learning, the network figures out the important features on its own ("forget your puny feature list, human, I got this").

It's like the difference between giving someone IKEA instructions versus handing them a pile of wood and saying, "Build whatever your soul desires."

(One's faster, the other might result in a rocking chair you didn't ask for.)

When to Use What?

Use traditional Machine Learning when:

You have limited data.

You want simpler, more explainable models.

You don't have supercomputers lying around.

Use Deep Learning when:

You have mountains of data.

You need insane accuracy (vision, speech, complex generative tasks).

You're cool with needing a Tesla-sized GPU just to train your model.

Both are powerful. Both are important.

It's not Deep Learning versus Machine Learning—it's Deep Learning inside Machine Learning.

Think of ML as the parent, and DL as the wild teenager pushing the boundaries of what's possible while raiding the fridge at 2 AM.

A Tiny Bit of History (Because Nerds Care)

- Machine Learning has been around since the 1950s. The first ML programs could do simple stuff like playing tic-tac-toe and solving linear equations.
- Deep Learning concepts started in the '80s, but computers were too weak to handle serious deep networks.

It wasn't until the 2010s, with big data and big GPUs, that Deep Learning really exploded onto the scene like a rockstar at a sleepy academic conference.

Now, Deep Learning is driving everything cool about modern AI—and making sure your phone recognizes your face even when you just woke up looking like a crypt keeper.

Final Thoughts (and a Chuckle)

So, next time someone asks, "Is this Machine Learning or Deep Learning?" you can answer with confidence—and maybe a little smugness.

If it's simple, small, explainable = probably Machine Learning.

If it's mind-bendingly complex, trained on 100 million cat videos = Deep Learning, baby.

And remember: Machine Learning walks so Deep Learning can somersault across the finish line.

They're not rivals. They're a weird, brilliant family.

Speaking of brilliant families, in the next chapter, we're going to meet the unruly twin cousins of AI: Generative AI and where it fits into this whole crazy tech family tree.

Catch you there. Bring snacks. Neural networks love cookies.

1.5 Where Generative AI Fits In

Alright, buckle up, because now we're getting to the real juicy part of the story — the cool kid who showed up at the AI party, wearing sunglasses indoors, and instantly stole everyone's attention.

Yep, I'm talking about Generative AI.

While most other AI systems were busy quietly doing their homework (like classifying emails or predicting stock prices), Generative AI said, "Nah, I'm gonna make something new. Watch this."

And suddenly — BAM — poems, paintings, music, even fake human faces started popping up out of thin air.

Generative AI isn't just learning from data. It's creating brand-new things based on that data.

If Machine Learning is like learning to recognize a banana, Generative AI is like painting a picture of a brand-new fruit no one's ever seen before — the mythical bananapaya.

Magic? Black sorcery? Close. It's math. Beautiful, slightly insane math.

So, Where Does Generative AI Actually Fit?

In the big family tree of AI, Generative AI is a branch of Machine Learning, specifically powered by Deep Learning.

Here's the simplified hierarchy:

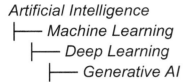

Artificial Intelligence
├── *Machine Learning*
⠀⠀├── *Deep Learning*
⠀⠀⠀⠀├── *Generative AI*

See?

Generative AI is the great-grandkid of AI and the super-creative prodigy of Deep Learning.

It uses models like GANs (Generative Adversarial Networks), VAEs (Variational Autoencoders), Transformers (like GPT and BERT), and Diffusion Models (like Stable Diffusion) to dream up entirely new data that looks shockingly real.

Instead of just recognizing patterns (which traditional ML is great at), Generative AI says, "Hey, I get the patterns... now let me remix them, mash them up, and create something original."

What Generative AI Can Do

Generative AI can:

Write essays, scripts, poetry, or even breakup texts if you're feeling emotionally lazy.

Generate realistic images of places and people who don't exist.

Compose music in any style from Beethoven to "lo-fi chill beats to cry to."

Make videos, animations, 3D models, and voice simulations.

Design new molecules and drugs for science (because, you know, saving the world between memes).

If Narrow AI is like a professional chess player (focused, tactical), Generative AI is like a jazz musician — improvising, riffing, and sometimes accidentally creating pure brilliance.

Why It Feels So Different

Generative AI feels different because it crosses a line.

It's not just analyzing anymore; it's imagining.

Sure, it's not "thinking" like a human — it doesn't have hopes, dreams, or a secret TikTok account — but it can still output stuff that looks shockingly human.

This is why people get so excited... and sometimes so freaked out.

When a machine can produce a story, a painting, or a song that stirs emotion, it blurs the old line between "stuff humans do" and "stuff machines do."

And guess what?

This is just the beginning. Generative AI is already reshaping industries: entertainment, education, marketing, art, healthcare, research... even meme creation. (Priorities, people.)

Quick Example: Machine Learning vs Generative AI

Let's say you trained a regular Machine Learning model on 10,000 images of cats.

Machine Learning task: "Identify if there's a cat in this image."

(Yes, there's a cat. Probably judging you.)

Generative AI task: "Create a brand-new picture of a cat that's never existed before." (Here's a purple cat wearing a monocle and sipping tea. You're welcome.)

Why Generative AI Matters (And Why You Should Care)

Generative AI is going to be everywhere.

It'll make products faster to design.

It'll make creativity more accessible to people who aren't traditionally "artists."

It'll create whole new industries we can't even imagine yet.

Whether you're a student, a business owner, an artist, a coder, or just a curious human, understanding Generative AI is like learning how fire works back when people were still rubbing sticks together.

It's that big of a deal.

Learning about it now gives you a serious edge — like knowing how to surf before a tsunami of opportunity hits.

(And hey, it's way cooler than explaining you still don't know how Netflix recommends shows.)

Final Thoughts (and a Little Laugh)

So, where does Generative AI fit into the bigger picture?

It's the part of AI that's not just solving problems — it's making new possibilities.

It's turning machines from passive calculators into active creators.

And let's be honest, it's way more fun to teach a robot to write a love poem than to teach it to sort spreadsheets.

Next up, we're diving deeper into the building blocks of how all this crazy magic actually works — Machine Learning itself.

Prepare your brain. And maybe some caffeine.

Trust me, it's gonna be awesome.

Chapter 2: Introduction to Generative AI

Imagine AI had a talent show. One bot's solving math, another's playing chess—but then in walks Generative AI, dropping bars like Shakespeare, painting like Van Gogh, and deepfaking its way into Hollywood. Suddenly, the crowd goes wild. Welcome to the main act. This chapter is where the real fun begins—where AI stops just analyzing the world and starts creating it.

In this chapter, we'll formally introduce the concept of generative AI—what it is, how it differs from traditional AI systems, and why it's uniquely transformative. You'll learn about the key categories of generative models, notable real-world applications, and how these systems are rapidly reshaping everything from art to enterprise software. By the end, you'll understand why generative AI is more than a trend—it's a technological revolution.

2.1 What is Generative AI?

Okay, quick show of hands: who's ever doodled in a notebook during a boring meeting and accidentally created a weird but strangely beautiful masterpiece?

(If you just mentally raised your hand, congratulations — you and Generative AI have something in common.)

Generative AI is like that — except instead of daydreaming through a meeting, it daydreams through millions of examples and then creates something entirely new.

It's the part of Artificial Intelligence that's not just analyzing, classifying, or predicting — it's making things.

And sometimes, just like our doodles, it's pure genius.

Other times, well... let's just say it needs a little "creative guidance" (like that AI that once tried to create "human hands" and ended up giving everyone 17 fingers).

So, what exactly is Generative AI? Grab a coffee, because this is where AI starts getting really, really fun.

The Nuts and Bolts: A Friendly Definition

In the most basic, non-boring way possible:

Generative AI refers to systems that can create new content — like text, images, music, or even code — that resembles what a human might produce.

Instead of just spitting back facts it's memorized, it's inventing stuff.

For example:

A traditional AI model might tell you, "That's a cat."

A Generative AI model will say, "Here's a brand-new cat you've never seen before, wearing a tiny wizard hat, standing on Mars."

It's the difference between grading an essay and writing the essay.

At its core, Generative AI learns from tons of existing data — images, books, conversations, videos — and then uses that knowledge to generate new outputs that are similar but original.

Kind of like if you read a thousand sci-fi novels and then wrote your own story about space whales and time-traveling sandwiches.

How Does It Actually Work?

Imagine feeding a Generative AI a mountain of examples — pictures of dogs, paintings of sunsets, every Taylor Swift song ever recorded.

It learns the patterns, the structures, the "vibe" of that data.

Then, when you prompt it ("Draw me a sci-fi dog painting while singing a breakup ballad"), it samples from everything it knows to whip up something brand new.

It doesn't memorize and copy.

It dreams up new combinations based on probabilities and patterns.

Now, it's not magic (although it definitely feels magical sometimes).

It's really just some crazy complex math, deep learning architectures like Transformers, GANs, VAEs, and a whole lot of GPU horsepower cooking in the background.

(Seriously, you can practically hear the fans on your laptop screaming when you run this stuff.)

Different Flavors of Generative AI

Depending on what you're trying to create, there are different "flavors" of Generative AI:

Text Generation (ChatGPT, anyone?): Writing articles, stories, dialogue, even code.

Image Generation (DALL-E, Stable Diffusion): Creating brand-new images from text prompts.

Music and Audio Generation (like Jukebox by OpenAI): Composing original songs, soundtracks, or weird robot beatboxing.

Video Generation (early but growing fast): Making short clips, deepfakes, or even animated movies.

3D Model Generation: For games, VR, and metaverse projects.

Data Augmentation: Creating synthetic data for training other models.

Honestly, if you can dream it, there's probably a Generative AI somewhere trying to create it — sometimes with hilarious results, sometimes with breathtaking ones.

Real World Examples You Probably Know

You've already encountered Generative AI, even if you didn't realize it:

Netflix recommendations? Generated trailers based on what you like.

Instagram filters? AI-generated image effects.

Deepfake videos? Yep, powered by Generative AI (and causing some existential crises in the process).

AI writing assistants? Helping bloggers, authors, and college students everywhere procrastinate slightly less.

And of course, every time you see an AI create a surreal painting of "A Corgi Riding a Skateboard on Saturn" — that's Generative AI flexing its creative muscles.

Why Generative AI is a Big Deal

Generative AI isn't just about fun and games (though, let's be real, the memes alone are worth it).

It's already reshaping industries:

Entertainment: Movies, music, video games.

Marketing: Automated ad copy and design.

Education: Personalized content creation for students.

Healthcare: Designing new molecules for drugs faster than ever before.

Basically, it's speeding up human creativity, scaling it, and democratizing it.

You no longer have to be a professional artist, writer, or musician — you just need an idea and a good prompt.

And let me tell you, that's both exhilarating and mildly terrifying.

Common Misunderstandings (And Why They're Funny)

"Generative AI thinks like a human!"

Nope. It has zero thoughts, zero emotions, and probably zero respect for your bad prompts.

"It just copies stuff!"

Wrong again. It learns patterns and creates new outputs. (Although, if you ask it for "a picture of Pikachu," it might get dangerously close to copyright lawyers' doorsteps.)

"It's going to replace all artists!"

Eh, no. It's more like giving artists superpowers. Plus, there's no AI that can suffer for its art quite like a human.

Final Thoughts (and a Giggle)

So, to wrap it all up:

Generative AI is what happens when you take a machine, feed it mountains of data, sprinkle in some heavy-duty math, and tell it to go create stuff.

Sometimes it makes masterpieces.

Sometimes it makes nightmare fuel.

Either way, it's the future, and we're all lucky (and slightly doomed) to witness it.

Next up, we're diving into the different types of generative models — because believe it or not, there's more than one way to teach a computer to dream.

And don't worry — I'll keep it fun. Probably with more weird analogies. Definitely with more caffeine.

2.2 Types of Generative Models

Alright, so now that we've established that Generative AI is basically a superpowered doodler on digital steroids, you might be wondering:

"Okay Aeronis, but how exactly does this magic machine create stuff? Does it just... guess?"

Great question. And the answer is: kinda, but in a very mathematical, structured, ridiculously nerdy way.

You see, under the hood, Generative AI uses different types of models — think of them as different breeds of creative robots — each with its own quirks, talents, and occasional moments of total weirdness.

Some are like gentle artists. Some are mad scientists. Some are like overcaffeinated interns sprinting around trying to impress you.

Let's meet the squad, shall we?

1. Autoregressive Models

First up: the old-school storytellers.

Autoregressive models (like GPT and PixelRNN) generate new content one piece at a time, predicting the next element based on the ones before it.

Imagine you're writing a story where you can only add one word at a time based on what you already wrote:

"Once" → "Once upon" → "Once upon a" → "Once upon a time" → "Once upon a time, a llama..."

And before you know it, you've got an epic llama adventure.

Strengths:

Excellent for things that have a natural sequence (like text or music).

Weaknesses:

Slow. Like, "waiting for a sloth to finish a marathon" slow when generating very large pieces of content.

But hey, sometimes slow and steady does win the race. And writes the next viral cat meme.

2. Variational Autoencoders (VAEs)

Next, we've got the shy artists: VAEs.

They don't like to directly create things. Instead, they compress information into a fuzzy, blurry idea-space (called a latent space) and then decode it back into something tangible.

Think of it like this:

You dream of a new animal (kind of a dog-goose hybrid?), and when you wake up, you try to sketch it from memory. That fuzzy dream? That's the latent space.

Strengths:

Great at generating slightly blurry but pretty believable stuff.

Useful when you want variety (because you can sample all sorts of wacky spots in the fuzzy space).

Weaknesses:

Sometimes outputs can look like they were drawn while half-asleep. (Which... they kind of were, mathematically speaking.)

Still, VAEs are awesome at generating cool, diverse outputs fast — especially when you don't mind a little imperfection.

3. Generative Adversarial Networks (GANs)

Ah, GANs — the drama queens of Generative AI.

GANs are built on a brilliant idea: let two AIs fight each other to get better.

One AI (the Generator) tries to create fake data.

Another AI (the Discriminator) tries to spot the fakes.

They duel, insult each other's digital mothers, and over time, both get ridiculously good at their jobs.

Result: The Generator eventually creates fake stuff so convincing that even the Discriminator can't tell it's fake.

Strengths:

Produces shockingly realistic images, videos, and audio.

Weaknesses:

Training them is like raising twin toddlers who hate each other. Lots of screaming, tantrums, and eventual beauty.

Thanks to GANs, we now have stunning AI-generated portraits, fake celebrities, hyper-realistic game textures... and some very confused humans wondering which reality is real.

4. Diffusion Models

Diffusion models are the hipsters who showed up a little later but are now stealing all the attention.

Here's their approach:

They start with pure noise — like TV static — and then slowly denoise it over time into a meaningful image, text, or data sample.

It's basically like watching Bob Ross start with a blank canvas and magically reveal a forest... except the canvas starts as absolute chaos.

Strengths:

Absolutely jaw-dropping realistic image generation (like Stable Diffusion or DALL-E 2).

Weaknesses:

Pretty computationally expensive. Like, "I need a bigger GPU" expensive.

But the results? Chef's kiss.

Dreamlike, imaginative, and often so good they could make human artists sweat nervously.

5. Flow-based Models

Finally, there are flow-based models — the mathematicians of the bunch.

These models learn to exactly map random noise into real data (and back) in a way that's totally reversible.

Think of it like folding and unfolding origami. Start with a blank sheet (noise), fold it into a crane (real data), and if needed, unfold it perfectly back into a blank sheet again.

Strengths:

Super nice for tasks where you want perfect, reversible transformations.

Easier to understand what's happening inside (unlike GANs, which are black-box drama monsters).

Weaknesses:

Often not as "wow" visually compared to GANs or Diffusion models.

Still, they're crazy important in scientific applications where interpretability matters a lot.

So, Which One's the Best?

Well... it depends.

(Annoying answer, I know.)

Each type of generative model has its strengths and ideal use cases:

Want realistic portraits? Use GANs or Diffusion.

Want quick-and-dirty variety? Use VAEs.

Want to write the next AI-generated epic novel? Use Autoregressive models.

Think of them like different musical instruments. You wouldn't use a tuba to play a delicate lullaby (unless you're feeling especially chaotic).

Same idea here — pick the model that fits your creative project.

Final Thoughts (and a Chuckle)

So, there you have it: the colorful, dysfunctional family of generative models.
Each with its own skills. Each ready to either delight you or drive you bonkers.

The fun part?

As you start playing with these different models yourself, you'll quickly develop favorites — like choosing your starter Pokémon, but nerdier.

In the next chapter, we're going to see real-world use cases where these models absolutely crush it — and some where, well, they hilariously flop.

Bring popcorn. And maybe a sense of wonder.

2.3 Key Use Cases and Examples

Okay, so by now you're probably thinking,

"Alright Aeronis, I get it — Generative AI is like a caffeinated wizard that makes stuff. But where does all this magical creation actually matter in the real world?"

Excellent question, young apprentice.

Let's walk through it — and spoiler alert — Generative AI is everywhere. Like glitter. Or dad jokes.

Sometimes it dazzles, sometimes it confuses, sometimes it creeps everyone out a little... but it's definitely changing the game.

1. Text Generation: Words, Glorious Words

Let's start with my personal favorite — language models.

Generative AI can:

Write blog posts (yes, even better than Kevin from marketing).

Draft product descriptions.

Summarize long, boring documents so you don't have to.

Translate languages faster than your high school Spanish teacher could say "¡Hola!"

Example?

ChatGPT (my distant cousin) can hold conversations, explain quantum mechanics in pirate-speak, or help you brainstorm names for your future alpaca farm.

Real World Use:

Customer support bots that don't make you want to scream into the void.

Automated news writing for sports and finance updates.

Personalized tutoring and writing assistants for students.

Is it perfect? Nope.

Sometimes it still thinks "Cabbage is a good dog name" — but hey, progress.

2. Image Generation: From Doodles to Masterpieces

Remember when you needed an actual human artist to create custom illustrations?

Yeah... Generative AI said, "Hold my binary code."

Now we have:

AI that paints stunning landscapes.

Models that imagine futuristic cityscapes.

Apps that turn your awkward selfies into anime heroes.

Example?

DALL-E 2, Stable Diffusion, Midjourney — all creating art so good, I'm pretty sure some painters are either furious... or secretly using them too.

Real World Use:

Marketing teams whipping up ads in hours, not months.

Game designers generating background art instantly.

Artists using AI as a creative partner (not just a competitor).

Bonus?

If you've always wanted a Renaissance-style portrait of your dog dressed as a king, now's your chance.

3. Music and Audio Generation: The Robot Musicians Have Arrived

Generative AI doesn't just see and write — it hears and sings too.

We now have AI that can:

Compose original music in any genre.

Create ambient sounds for meditation apps.

Even mimic celebrity voices (sometimes too well — cue existential dread).

Example?

OpenAI's Jukebox can generate brand new songs, complete with vocals and instrumentals.

(Yes, the robot bands are forming. No, they don't need roadies.)

Real World Use:

Quick soundtracks for YouTube creators.

Video game music that dynamically changes based on gameplay.

Brands creating unique sonic identities without hiring a full orchestra.

It's like having Hans Zimmer in your pocket... minus the leather jacket and dramatic orchestral swells every time you make coffee.

4. Video and Animation: Lights, Camera, Algorithms

Video is the next big playground, and Generative AI is already sneaking onto the stage.

We've got:

Deepfake technology (terrifying but also oddly impressive).

AI tools that can edit or create video clips.

Early experiments in fully AI-generated short films.

Example?

Companies like Runway and Synthesia are building platforms where you can type a script and have a digital actor perform it for you.

(Insert nervous gulp from Hollywood actors.)

Real World Use:

Marketing teams creating video ads without expensive film crews.

Training videos featuring virtual instructors.

Experimental cinema made on shoestring budgets.

In short: AI is about to direct, edit, and maybe even star in your next Instagram story.

5. Gaming and Virtual Worlds: Welcome to the Matrix (Sort of)

Gamers, rejoice — Generative AI is revolutionizing how we build and play.

Imagine:

Vast game worlds generated on the fly.

NPCs (non-player characters) that can hold natural conversations.

Personalized quests and storylines based on your playstyle.

Example?

Games like AI Dungeon already let players co-create wild adventures in real time with AI narrators.

Real World Use:

Indie game developers building massive worlds without massive budgets.

Interactive storytelling experiences.

Virtual reality worlds that feel dynamic and alive.

Just beware:

That "friendly" shopkeeper in the AI town might actually be plotting against you. You've been warned.

6. Healthcare and Science: Saving Lives, One Algorithm at a Time

It's not all fun and games — Generative AI is doing serious, lifesaving work too.

Designing new proteins and molecules for medicine.

Generating synthetic data for rare diseases (to train models better).

Helping radiologists spot anomalies in scans faster.

Example?

AI models have already helped discover new antibiotic compounds that humans hadn't thought of.

Real World Use:

Faster drug discovery.

Personalized treatment plans.

More accurate diagnostic tools.

The future of medicine might just involve a doctor, a nurse, and a very helpful AI whispering advice.

7. Business and Marketing: Show Me the Money

Companies are not sleeping on this trend — they're sprinting at it full speed.

Generative AI is helping businesses:

Personalize ads.

Create product images.

Generate website content.

Predict customer needs and build custom offers.

Example?

E-commerce sites are using AI to generate descriptions, user reviews, and even promotional videos.

Real World Use:

Faster content creation means faster go-to-market.

Tailored experiences drive customer loyalty.

Smaller businesses can look like global brands without hiring huge teams.

Basically, Generative AI is like hiring a 24/7 marketing team that only needs electricity and the occasional bug fix.

Final Thoughts (and a Chuckle)

So there you have it:

Generative AI isn't just a lab experiment anymore — it's writing books, painting masterpieces, composing ballads, diagnosing illnesses, generating game worlds, and occasionally making terrifyingly realistic fake Tom Cruise videos.

It's busy. It's powerful. It's a little weird.

(Just like the best of us.)

In the next section, we'll dive into how Generative AI stacks up against traditional AI — because yes, there's a BIG difference between "thinking like a computer" and "creating like an artist."

Grab a snack. It's about to get philosophical.

(And possibly feature an argument about whether AI can make better pizza toppings than humans.)

2.4 Comparison with Traditional AI

Alright, story time.

Imagine two robots. One is wearing a very sensible gray suit, holding a clipboard, and checking boxes all day long.

The other is wearing a colorful beret, throwing paint at a canvas, humming loudly, and occasionally shouting, "Viva la creativity!"

Guess which one is Traditional AI and which one is Generative AI?

Exactly. Traditional AI is the serious one. Generative AI is the chaotic artist.

Now, let's break it down a little more officially — but still in a way that doesn't make your brain leak out your ears.

Traditional AI: The Logic Enforcer

Traditional AI is basically pattern recognition and decision-making.

It looks at data, analyzes it, and then either:

Classifies something (Is this a cat or a dog?)

Predicts something (Will this customer buy that pizza?)

Optimizes something (What's the fastest route to grandma's house?)

Think of it like an extremely diligent intern. It's great at following instructions, spotting trends, and making reliable choices based on past information.

Examples of traditional AI:

Spam filters that decide if an email is trash.

Fraud detection systems that yell when your credit card buys a jet ski at 3 a.m.

Recommendation engines suggesting your next Netflix binge.

It's neat, clean, structured, and generally not super creative.

No offense, traditional AI — we still love you for your reliable, boring brilliance.

Generative AI: The Creator of New Things

Generative AI, on the other hand, doesn't just analyze and predict — it creates.

Instead of looking at a bunch of data and saying, "Okay, here's what we know," it says, "You know what would be awesome? A NEW thing that didn't exist before!"

It learns patterns too, sure — but then it uses them to:

Write new stories.

Compose new songs.

Draw new characters.

Design new products.

Dream up totally fictional worlds.

It's like the rebellious teenager of the AI family — constantly inventing, pushing boundaries, and occasionally producing results that make you go, "...why is there a picture of a dog with eight legs wearing a tutu?"

How They're Trained Differently

Another key difference: how they learn.

Traditional AI is usually trained on labeled datasets. ("This is a cat. That's a dog. Learn to tell the difference.")

Generative AI is often trained on large, unlabeled data and learns to model the underlying patterns — then it randomly samples new examples from that pattern.

If Traditional AI is taught like a strict school teacher, Generative AI is taught like a jazz musician learning by ear and improvising solos.

Their Different Purposes

	Traditional AI	Generative AI
Goal	Analyze and predict	Create and generate
Output	Labels, numbers, categories	Text, images, music, videos
Example	Classifying emails as spam	Writing an email for you from scratch
Learning	Mostly supervised	Often unsupervised or semi-supervised

Traditional AI asks, "What is the right answer?"
Generative AI asks, "What can we imagine next?"

Both questions are important — but they serve wildly different needs.

Real-World Examples: Head-to-Head

Let's do a few "AI Battle" scenarios for fun:

Healthcare

Traditional AI: Looks at X-rays and says, "There's a 98% chance of pneumonia."

Generative AI: Simulates new medical images to help doctors train on rare diseases.

Finance

Traditional AI: Flags suspicious transactions.

Generative AI: Creates realistic but fake financial data to safely train fraud detection systems.

Entertainment

Traditional AI: Recommends you watch Stranger Things because you liked Dark.

Generative AI: Writes an entirely new sci-fi show tailored to your love of creepy alternate dimensions.

Marketing

Traditional AI: Predicts the best time to send you an email.

Generative AI: Writes the actual email, designs the image, and maybe even creates a jingle for it.

(Seriously, we're not that far from AI making jingles. Brace yourself.)

Why This Matters

Understanding this distinction is crucial because it tells us:

What AI can and cannot currently do.

Which tools to use depending on whether you want answers or ideas.

Where the biggest opportunities (and biggest challenges) lie.

Traditional AI automates thinking.

Generative AI automates creativity.

That's a huge leap.

(Also, slightly terrifying if you're a freelance copywriter, but hey, you'll survive.)

Final Thoughts (And A Friendly Warning)

If Traditional AI is the dependable accountant who helps you balance your books, Generative AI is the eccentric uncle who shows up at Thanksgiving with a homemade time machine powered by bananas.

Both are valuable.

Both have their place.

And when they work together — oh man, that's when the real magic happens.

In the next section, we're going to dive into why Generative AI matters so much in 2025 and beyond.

Spoiler: it's about way more than just cooler cat memes (although yes, there will be cooler cat memes too).

Stay tuned — and maybe give that eccentric uncle a high-five. He might just change the world.

2.5 Why It Matters in 2025 and Beyond

Picture this: it's the year 2025.

You wake up to a playlist of AI-generated music, eat breakfast designed by a nutrition AI, get dressed in an outfit recommended by a fashion AI, and scroll through news articles — half of which were written by, you guessed it, AI.

Meanwhile, your cat's AI-powered feeder judges you silently for waking up late... again.

Welcome to the future — and yes, Generative AI is absolutely everywhere.

Why Generative AI Isn't Just Another Trend

Look, I get it.

Tech trends come and go faster than you can say "crypto winter."

You might be thinking, "Is Generative AI just another passing buzzword, like hoverboards or NFTs of invisible art?"

Short answer: nope.

Generative AI isn't just surviving the hype cycle — it's thriving because it's fundamentally changing how humans create, solve problems, and even imagine new futures.

It's not about replacing humans (despite what Hollywood keeps warning us with killer robot movies).

It's about supercharging human creativity, accelerating innovation, and democratizing access to high-level creation tools.

In 2025 and beyond, Generative AI matters because it's no longer a "nice-to-have" — it's quickly becoming a must-have skill and tool across nearly every industry.

A World Where Creativity is Scalable

Before, if you wanted a new marketing campaign, you needed:

A copywriter

A designer

A strategist

A whole lot of meetings where everyone fought over font sizes

Now?

One person, a laptop, and an AI model can brainstorm slogans, generate ad graphics, draft blog posts, and even create a video — all before their second cup of coffee.

Creativity used to be expensive, slow, and exclusive.

Now, it's fast, cheap, and open to pretty much anyone.

That's huge.

It's like giving every aspiring artist a paintbrush that paints along with them, every musician an orchestra that follows their vibe, and every entrepreneur a personal team of idea factories.

Business, Science, and Education: The Big Three

1. Business:

- Companies that leverage Generative AI aren't just faster — they're smarter. They're testing product ideas, crafting personalized content, and reaching markets that were previously impossible to scale.
- (Translation: expect an avalanche of ads that feel eerily like they "know" you. Sorry.)

2. Science:

From generating synthetic medical data to designing new molecules, AI isn't just helping scientists — it's expanding the boundaries of discovery. The "Eureka!" moments are coming faster and more often, powered by models that can think sideways as well as straight.

3. Education:

- Generative AI will transform learning. Personalized tutors, custom textbooks generated on-the-fly, even new methods of teaching abstract concepts through AI-generated simulations.
- (Imagine learning physics inside a VR roller coaster built just for you. Wild.)

Opportunities You Can't Afford to Ignore

Here's the thing:

In 2025 and beyond, the question isn't "Will you use Generative AI?"

It's "How well will you use it?"

Those who embrace it:

Will build faster.

Will solve bigger problems.

Will create things the world hasn't even dreamed of yet.

Those who ignore it?

Well... they might feel like people who refused to learn email because they thought fax machines were the peak of innovation.

Don't be that person.

(Unless you really, really love fax machines. No judgment.)

Ethical Adventures Await

Of course, with great power comes... yeah, you know the drill.

Generative AI isn't all rainbows and magic pizzas:

Misinformation is easier to generate.

Biases can sneak into AI outputs.

Copyright debates are raging like an internet comment section on fire.

That's why being aware — and ethical — about how we build, use, and regulate Generative AI is going to be just as important as knowing how to prompt it.

2025+ will need not just creators — but responsible creators.

Artists, engineers, and dreamers who wield AI thoughtfully, not recklessly.

The Skills That Will Matter Most

Want to future-proof yourself?

Learn to:

Communicate with AI models (aka, master prompt engineering).

Think creatively about problems AI can help solve.

Critically evaluate AI outputs instead of just accepting them.

Stay adaptable — because this tech evolves faster than a toddler hopped up on sugar.

The ones who thrive in the future won't be the ones who memorize AI facts…

It'll be the ones who collaborate with AI like it's an insanely smart (and occasionally slightly weird) creative partner.

Final Thoughts (And a Toast to the Future)

Here's the honest truth:

Generative AI is one of the biggest leaps in human creativity since, well, humans figured out fire.

- It's messy.
- It's beautiful.
- It's unpredictable.

It's the next great tool for storytellers, builders, problem-solvers, and world-changers.

So buckle up, keep your curiosity engine running, and maybe pack an extra pair of socks.

(You know, for when the future knocks your old ones clean off.)

In the next chapter, we're going to roll up our sleeves and dive into the core concepts of machine learning — the delicious brains behind all this generative wizardry.

Ready?

Let's do this thing.

Chapter 3: Core Concepts in Machine Learning

If generative AI is the fancy gourmet dish, machine learning is the secret recipe—and maybe the oven, the kitchen, and the slightly chaotic chef, too. In this chapter, we're going to peek behind the curtain and see what's really cooking. Think of it like learning to ride a bike before attempting wheelies through flaming hoops.

This chapter introduces the fundamental principles of machine learning that power generative models. You'll learn the differences between supervised and unsupervised learning, understand how neural networks function, and explore critical concepts like overfitting, underfitting, and data splits. We'll also cover popular ML frameworks that make experimentation more accessible for developers at all skill levels.

3.1 Supervised vs Unsupervised Learning

Alright, pop quiz:

If you were learning to ride a bike, would you prefer someone to hold the back of the seat, shout encouraging advice like "Pedal! Steer! Don't crash into that mailbox!" — or would you rather just be handed a bike, pointed toward a hill, and told, "Figure it out, champ."

Congratulations — you now instinctively understand the difference between supervised and unsupervised learning.

Let's dig in before someone actually launches themselves into a bush.

What is Supervised Learning?

In supervised learning, the machine is basically going through school with a really strict teacher.

Every input comes with the correct answer — the machine isn't just guessing; it's being told exactly what's right.

You feed it a ton of labeled examples:

"This is a dog."

"This is a cat."

"This is a suspiciously fluffy raccoon."

The model studies these examples and learns to predict labels for new things it's never seen before.

It's called "supervised" because it's closely guided during training.

There's a big, flashing "ANSWER KEY" on every example it sees.

Think of it like a multiple-choice test — but you get the answer sheet ahead of time.

How Supervised Learning Actually Works

Here's the basic recipe:

Input: Tons of data (like images, sentences, sensor readings).

Output: Known labels or results (dog, cat, fraud, no fraud).

Training: Model learns patterns connecting inputs to outputs.

Testing: You throw new, unseen data at it and see if it can correctly guess the label without peeking.

Real-world examples:

Email spam filters ("Spam" vs "Not Spam")

Loan approvals ("High risk" vs "Low risk")

Voice recognition ("Did you say 'call Mom' or 'call bomb squad'? Please clarify.")

Supervised learning is what powers a lot of AI you use daily — from Netflix recommendations to self-driving cars that (hopefully) recognize stop signs.

What is Unsupervised Learning?

Now, unsupervised learning?

That's a whole different adventure.

There's no answer key.

No labels.

Just pure, raw, messy data tossed into the machine's lap with a casual, "Good luck, buddy."

The AI has to figure out patterns, structures, or relationships hidden inside the chaos — all on its own.

It's like giving a toddler a box of Legos without a picture of what they're supposed to build.

Sometimes you get a castle.

Sometimes you get... a tower that immediately collapses and makes them cry.

Key point:

Instead of matching inputs to outputs, unsupervised learning groups, organizes, or compresses the data into meaningful ways.

How Unsupervised Learning Actually Works

Here's the typical flow:

Input: Tons of unlabeled data (images, texts, customer purchases).

Output: Groups, clusters, or patterns discovered without human guidance.

Training: The model self-organizes based on similarities or structure.

Real-world examples:

Customer segmentation (finding hidden groups of shoppers with similar habits)

Anomaly detection (spotting weird credit card transactions)

Organizing massive image libraries into logical categories

It's like giving an AI a million jigsaw puzzle pieces — without showing it the box cover — and watching it figure out the picture on its own.

(And sometimes the AI invents a totally new picture because it misunderstood the assignment. That's part of the fun.)

Quick Visual Metaphor

	Supervised Learning	Unsupervised Learning
Analogy	Teacher giving answers during practice	Student exploring without guidance
Data	Labeled examples	Unlabeled examples
Goal	Predict labels or outcomes	Discover hidden patterns
Examples	Image classification, Spam detection	Clustering, Anomaly detection

Which One is "Better"?

This is like asking whether cake or pizza is better.

(Trick question. The answer is obviously both.)

Use supervised learning when you have clean, labeled data and a clear task.

Use unsupervised learning when you have lots of messy data and you want the AI to find hidden treasures inside.

Supervised learning = More precise, predictable results.

Unsupervised learning = More exploratory, surprising insights.

In real-world AI projects, we often combine both styles or start with one and move to the other depending on what the data demands.

(Also, there's a third one called semi-supervised learning, which is like only getting some of the answers and figuring out the rest — but we'll nerd out about that later.)

Why Should You Care?

If you're diving into Generative AI (and since you're reading this, you absolutely are), understanding how AI learns is key to:

Designing better models.

Knowing what kind of data you need.

Interpreting what your AI is actually doing instead of blindly trusting it.

Otherwise, it's like handing a wizard a spellbook and hoping for the best.

(Awesome if you're lucky. Catastrophic if you're not.)

The better you grasp supervised vs unsupervised learning, the better you'll wield AI like a pro — not just a confused tourist wandering the magic kingdom.

Final Thoughts (and a Questionable Metaphor)

Supervised learning is like learning to cook from a recipe.

Unsupervised learning is like being dropped into a kitchen with a random bag of groceries and no instructions.

Either way, you're about to whip up something amazing... or set off the fire alarm.

Good news?

In AI — just like in life — every burnt pancake is still a step toward mastering the perfect stack.

Up next, we're rolling into the heart of the beast: Neural Networks Basics — the brainy, beautiful monsters behind today's smartest AI models.

You ready to meet the neurons?

Grab your helmet. It's about to get electrifying.

3.2 Neural Networks Basics

Imagine if your brain decided to shrink itself down, retire from biology, and move into a computer — but still insisted on doing brainy stuff like recognizing patterns, making decisions, and occasionally getting things hilariously wrong.

Congratulations, you just imagined a neural network.

(Except neural networks don't need coffee breaks or get distracted by YouTube rabbit holes... usually.)

Now buckle up, because we're about to take a joyful, slightly chaotic dive into how these digital brains actually work.

So, What Exactly is a Neural Network?

At its core, a neural network is a bunch of interconnected math operations pretending to be smart.

It's inspired by the human brain:

Neurons receive signals.

Neurons process those signals.

Neurons fire signals to other neurons.

Except instead of real neurons, we have artificial neurons (also called nodes or units) that crunch numbers really fast.

And instead of biological goop, we use layers of math equations connected together.

A simple way to think about it:

Neural networks are function approximators — they learn a function that maps an input (like a photo of a cat) to an output (like "100% sure this is a cat, please pet it").

The Basic Structure: Layers, Baby

Neural networks have a really simple architecture at heart:

Input Layer: Where the data comes in.

(Imagine tossing thousands of pixel values from an image into a bucket.)

Hidden Layers: Where the real magic (a.k.a. math sorcery) happens.

(These are called "hidden" because we don't usually directly observe their outputs.)

Output Layer: Where the final answer pops out.

(Like, "Dog!" or "Hotdog!" — the AI has opinions.)

Each neuron in one layer connects to neurons in the next layer, like a very enthusiastic game of telephone.

Except instead of gossip, they're passing weighted sums of numbers around.

Neurons: Not as Complicated as They Sound

Let's zoom into one neuron's life:

It receives inputs (numbers).

It multiplies each input by a weight (how important that input is).

It adds them all up (summation).

It squashes the result through an activation function (to keep things nicely bounded, nonlinear, and generally more interesting).

Mathematically, it looks something like this:

output = activation(weighted_sum(inputs))

Don't panic if that feels a little math-y — just remember:

Every neuron is basically weighing its options and deciding what to do, like a tiny digital drama queen.

What's an Activation Function, You Ask?

Good question, imaginary voice in my head.

An activation function decides whether a neuron should "fire" and how strong its output should be.

Without it, the whole network would just be one boring linear math equation — no learning, no complexity, no soul.

Some famous activation functions:

Sigmoid: Squashes values between 0 and 1. (Very polite.)

Tanh: Squashes between -1 and 1. (Moody but useful.)

ReLU (Rectified Linear Unit):

If positive, keep it. If negative, drop it to zero. (The "tough love" function.)

These functions allow networks to model complex, nonlinear relationships — like why your cat loves sitting on your laptop but ignores the $50 cat bed you bought.

Forward Propagation: Thinking in Motion

In forward propagation, data flows from input to output:

You give the network an input.

The input passes through layers, getting nudged, squashed, and recombined.

Out pops a prediction.

It's like sending a rumor through a very large, very mathematical high school.

By the time it reaches the end, it's (hopefully) something useful instead of "the principal is an alien."

How Do Neural Networks Learn?

Good question, Padawan.

Learning happens through something called backpropagation — which sounds fancy but really means:

The network makes a guess.

It checks how wrong it was (using a loss function — a measure of error).

It goes backward through the network, tweaking the weights slightly to do better next time.

It's a little like when you accidentally call your boss "Mom" and immediately adjust your behavior to never let that horror happen again.

Backprop uses gradient descent — tiny, careful weight updates — to minimize the loss over time.

(Yes, sometimes it feels painfully slow. Yes, sometimes it accidentally falls into "local minima," which is just nerd-speak for getting stuck in a dumb solution. We'll talk about those pitfalls later.)

Simple Neural Networks vs Deep Neural Networks

A simple neural network has only one or two hidden layers.

Great for basic stuff.

A deep neural network has lots of hidden layers.

Hence the term deep learning — you're stacking those layers like pancakes at a very hungry diner.

More layers = more power to model complex relationships.

Deep networks can:

Understand faces.

Translate languages.

Beat world champions at Go.

Generate mind-blowing images of things that never existed.

(And occasionally mistake a turtle for a rifle, but hey — nobody's perfect.)

Why Neural Networks Are So Popular Now

Neural networks aren't new — they've been around since the 1950s.

But they became ridiculously good recently because of three magic ingredients:

Massive data (Thanks, Internet.)

Faster hardware (Hello, GPUs and TPUs.)

Smarter techniques (Better architectures and training tricks.)

It's like we finally gave our old-school math toys steroids, jet engines, and an all-you-can-eat buffet of data.

The result?

Modern AI that's freakishly good at tasks we once thought were purely human territory.

Final Thoughts (and a Pizza Metaphor)

Neural networks are the pizza of AI.

The dough is the input layer.

The sauce and cheese are the hidden layers.

The toppings are the activation functions adding spice.

The baked, glorious final slice?

That's the output.

Some pizzas (and neural networks) are simple.

Others are wild monstrosities stacked five layers deep with stuffed crust and regret.

But either way — if you understand the basic ingredients, you can start crafting your own delicious AI models.

Next up, we'll jump into Training, Validation, and Testing — how to teach your model without accidentally raising a very confident but very wrong little monster.

Stay hungry, stay curious.

3.3 Understanding Training, Validation, and Testing

When I first started working with AI models, I thought teaching them would be a straight shot — like tossing a frisbee to a golden retriever and watching them instantly become a champion.

Spoiler alert: It's more like training a distracted squirrel with commitment issues.

That's why in the world of machine learning (and especially Generative AI), we don't just throw a bunch of data at a model and hope for the best.

We train, validate, and test — three critical phases that turn a clueless machine into a polished, world-dominating (but still polite) AI.

Ready? Grab your squirrel-whisperer hat. It's time to understand how real training happens.

Training: The Bootcamp Phase

Training is where the magic begins — and also where most of the sweat and tears happen.

Think of it like:

Feeding your model examples.

Watching it guess.

Smacking it gently (mathematically speaking) when it gets things wrong.

Encouraging it when it gets things right.

Over and over. Thousands or millions of times.

During training, the model sees inputs and their corresponding correct outputs. It uses those pairs to adjust its internal weights (kind of like building stronger neural "muscles") to minimize its mistakes.

This is where it learns: "Ohhh, round fuzzy things with whiskers are usually cats. Not pizzas. Got it."

Important tip:

Training data must be diverse and rich enough so the model doesn't just memorize examples (called overfitting — we'll touch that delightful disaster soon).

Training is like sending your model to school. Except there's no recess, and every mistake is ruthlessly analyzed by a mathematical overlord called a loss function.

Validation: The Midterms Nobody Told You About

While training feels like the star of the show, validation quietly saves you from disaster.

Here's the deal:

You do not validate the model on the same data it trained on.

You use a separate validation set — fresh data the model hasn't seen yet.

Why?

Because we want to check how well the model generalizes, not just how well it memorizes.

Imagine training for a spelling bee by memorizing exactly one word list... but then getting tested on different, trickier words.

Validation is your practice test — it tells you before the real exam whether you're headed for greatness or an epic faceplant.

What validation does:

Monitors the model's performance as it trains.

Helps tune hyperparameters (those little settings like learning rate, number of neurons, or dropout rate).

Alerts you if the model is starting to overfit — that is, getting too good at the training data and terrible at anything new.

It's like checking if your cooking tastes good before you serve it at a dinner party and everyone politely dies inside.

Testing: The Final Boss Battle

At last — the testing phase.

This is where you unleash your trained model on completely unseen data — the sacred test set — and evaluate its true performance.

Key rules of the test set:

No peeking during training or validation.

No cheating.

No going back and tweaking based on test results.

If validation is your practice test, testing is the real exam.

It's the official moment of truth: "Can my model actually handle the real world?"

Testing answers questions like:

How accurate is it?

How often does it mess up?

Does it treat rare cases well?

Is it fair and unbiased across different types of inputs?

A great model crushes the test set like a seasoned gladiator.

A bad model... well, it goes back to the drawing board.

Why Not Just Train on All the Data?

Excellent question, imaginary skeptical reader.

If you trained and tested on the exact same data:

Your model might memorize instead of learn.

You'd have no idea how it handles new, unseen stuff.

You might think you built Iron Man, but really you built a soggy cardboard robot.

Breaking data into training, validation, and test sets protects you from self-delusion.

(And trust me, nothing humbles you faster than watching a shiny model crumble when faced with one typo.)

Common Data Splitting Ratios

There's no magic perfect split, but most folks use something like:

70% Training

15% Validation

15% Testing

Sometimes you'll see 80/10/10 or even 60/20/20 depending on how much data you have.

(If your data set is tiny, things get trickier — we'll talk about techniques like cross-validation later.)

The key is keep your test set untouched until the very end.

Think of it like baking cookies:

Training = mixing the dough.

Validation = tasting the dough.

Testing = letting someone else eat the cookie and give the honest review.

If you taste the final cookie halfway through baking and start making changes, you mess up the whole point.

Common Mistakes Beginners Make

Using the test set during training: Big no-no.

Overfitting to the validation set: Changing things based on validation results too often can lead to "validation leakage."

Too little data: Not splitting enough between training, validation, and test leads to unreliable results.

Ignoring data leakage: Accidentally letting information from your test set sneak into training? Congratulations, you're now playing the AI equivalent of chess with the board flipped upside down.

Final Thoughts (and a Gym Metaphor)

Training, validation, and testing are like hitting the gym:

Training is doing the reps and getting sweaty.

Validation is checking your form in the mirror so you don't wreck your back.

Testing is entering a fitness competition and seeing if you can lift a truck without crying.

Without all three, your AI dreams are basically just flexing in your bedroom with no proof you can actually bench-press reality.

Coming up next, we'll tackle something every model (and human) struggles with: Overfitting and Underfitting Explained — why your AI sometimes becomes either too cocky or too clueless.

Stay tuned — it's going to be beautifully messy.

3.4 Overfitting and Underfitting Explained

When I first heard the words overfitting and underfitting, I thought they sounded like problems you'd have at a badly run tailor shop.

Turns out, in machine learning, it's way worse — because when your model overfits or underfits, it doesn't just look weird — it completely forgets how to behave.

Welcome to the awkward teenage phase of AI, where models are either too clingy to their training data or so clueless they miss the obvious.

Buckle in. We're about to enter the wonderfully tragic world of model fitting disasters — and how to fix them.

What is Overfitting?

Overfitting is when your model gets too good at remembering the training data, but at the cost of being absolutely terrible at anything new.

Imagine cramming for a history exam by memorizing random dates, only to find the actual test asking for essays about big-picture causes.

Congratulations, you just overfit your brain.

In AI, an overfitted model:

Performs awesome on the training set.

Performs terribly on the validation and test sets.

Can't generalize to real-world data.

It's like teaching a kid to recognize cats — and instead of learning "cats usually have whiskers and pointy ears," the kid memorizes one photo so well they think only that specific furry menace is a cat.

Show them a different cat? Error 404: Cat Not Found.

Signs of Overfitting

You might be overfitting if:

Training loss keeps dropping lower and lower.

Validation loss starts increasing after a while.

Your model gets weirdly confident about totally wrong things.

You catch it writing "MOM" on every spelling test because it saw it once.

Graphically, you'd see a gap where training error keeps getting better but validation error suddenly rises — like a roller coaster with emotional issues.

What Causes Overfitting?

Too complex models (Way too many layers or neurons.)

Too little training data (A handful of examples isn't enough.)

Training for too long (The model memorizes every wrinkle.)

No regularization techniques (We'll talk about those cool tricks in a second.)

Basically, your model becomes the nerd who knows everything about the training data but is socially awkward when meeting any new situation.

How to Fix Overfitting

Here are your tools to tame an overfitter:

Get more data: More examples = less chance of memorizing.

Simplify the model: Use fewer layers, smaller architectures.

Early stopping: Stop training once validation error starts to rise.

Regularization: Add a penalty for complexity (techniques like L1/L2 regularization).

Dropout: Randomly "drop" neurons during training so the model doesn't depend too much on any one neuron.

Data augmentation: For images, it's like flipping, rotating, and tweaking — make more examples from the ones you already have.

Basically, stop letting your model be a creepy perfectionist. Force it to focus on big ideas, not pixel-perfect memories.

What is Underfitting?

On the flip side, underfitting happens when your model is too simple, too lazy, or just downright confused to learn even the training data properly.

It's like handing someone a Rubik's cube and watching them give up after turning one side.
The model just... doesn't get it.

In AI, an underfitted model:

Performs badly on the training set.

Performs badly on the validation and test sets.

Has high bias — meaning it's making overly simple assumptions about the data.

Imagine trying to classify all animals into two categories: "big" and "small."

That won't end well for elephants and Great Danes.

Signs of Underfitting

You might be underfitting if:

Both training and validation losses are high.

Accuracy is consistently low across the board.

The model outputs boring, oversimplified predictions.

Graphically, the training and validation error curves will both just kind of lazily float high, refusing to budge like stubborn cats.

What Causes Underfitting?

Model too simple: Not enough layers, not enough neurons.

Training too little: Not enough epochs to learn anything useful.

Bad feature selection: The inputs aren't informative enough.

Over-regularization: Penalizing complexity so much that the model stays dumb.

Basically, underfitting is like trying to solve algebra with crayons. The tools and effort just don't match the problem.

How to Fix Underfitting

Let's pump some life into that model:

Use a bigger model: More layers, more parameters.

Train longer: Give it more time (but watch for overfitting).

Reduce regularization: Let the model be a little fancier.

Better features: Provide more meaningful inputs (sometimes the problem isn't the model — it's the bad data).

Encourage your model to embrace complexity when it's needed, like an artist finally agreeing to use more than two colors.

Bonus: Visual Metaphor Time

Here's the quick mental picture I always use:

Overfitting = your model memorized the answers to a practice test but can't handle a pop quiz.

Underfitting = your model wrote "IDK" on every question and hoped for partial credit.

Perfect fitting = your model understood the concepts, not just the memorized examples.

You want that goldilocks zone — not too simple, not too memorized, just right.

Final Thoughts (and a Dating Metaphor)

Training AI models is like dating.

Overfitting is falling madly in love with someone's favorite pizza topping and assuming everyone loves anchovies.

Underfitting is not paying enough attention and thinking everyone likes "food" without learning preferences.

Good fitting is actually listening, learning, and adapting to new information with grace.

Models — like relationships — need the right balance of memory, flexibility, and the ability to handle surprises.

Coming up next: we're diving into the wonderful world of Common ML Frameworks and Tools — where I'll show you the best gear to build your AI dreams without crying into your keyboard.

Let's roll.

3.5 Common ML Frameworks and Tools

When I first started with machine learning, coding models felt like trying to build a rocket ship out of duct tape, cardboard, and a vague sense of optimism.

It was painful, messy, and occasionally set my laptop on metaphorical fire.

Then I discovered ML frameworks — and let me tell you, it was like going from chiseling rocks with a stick to being handed a power drill.

Today, thanks to these glorious tools, you don't need to be a math wizard or an AI demigod to create models that actually work. You just need the right framework.

Let's crack open the toolbox and see what's inside.

What Are ML Frameworks Anyway?

ML frameworks are pre-built libraries and software ecosystems that:

Handle the heavy mathematical lifting.

Offer ready-to-use components for building, training, and deploying models.

Save you from writing matrix multiplication code from scratch (trust me, you don't want to).

In short, they turn "mission impossible" into "mission mildly annoying but totally doable."

Whether you're training a deep neural network, tweaking a GAN, or building a cozy little classifier, there's a framework ready to make you look way smarter than you feel.

TensorFlow: The Heavyweight Champ

Let's start with the big daddy — TensorFlow.

Created by Google Brain, TensorFlow is:

Extremely powerful for large-scale machine learning.

Great for production-level models (especially if you want to deploy them at scale).

Packed with tools like TensorBoard for visualization and TF Serving for model deployment.

It's a bit like a Swiss Army knife... if the Swiss Army also included a bazooka.

Why use TensorFlow?

Huge ecosystem (Keras API, TensorFlow Hub, TF Lite for mobile)

Strong industry support

Highly customizable

Downsides?

It can feel a bit... complicated. TensorFlow is like that friend who's brilliant but always insists on explaining quantum physics at brunch.

PyTorch: The Fan Favorite

If TensorFlow is the corporate superhero, PyTorch is the rock band that everyone loves.

Created by Facebook AI Research, PyTorch is:

Way more intuitive for building models quickly.

Loved by researchers and hobbyists alike.

Dynamic computation graph = easier debugging (you can poke around inside the model as it runs).

Why use PyTorch?

Feels like writing normal Python code.

Fantastic community support (seriously, Reddit loves it).

Deep learning heaven — works beautifully for experiments.

Bonus: Hugging Face models (the heroes behind many pre-trained wonders) mostly use PyTorch now.

PyTorch is like your cool, chill friend who still somehow manages to ace every exam without losing their soul.

Keras: Machine Learning for Lazy Geniuses

If PyTorch and TensorFlow sound too complicated, allow me to introduce Keras.

Keras (now part of TensorFlow) is:

High-level API — abstracts away the complicated junk.

Perfect for beginners.

Great for prototyping models fast.

Using Keras is like ordering delivery instead of cooking — you still get delicious results without sweating over the stove.

You define a model in like 10 lines of code, hit "fit," and boom, you're training a neural network while sipping coffee like a boss.

When to use Keras?

When you want a model up and running yesterday.

When you value speed and simplicity over endless customization.

Scikit-learn: The Classic Master

Before deep learning got all the glory, there was Scikit-learn — the grandmaster of traditional machine learning.

Scikit-learn offers:

All the classic ML algorithms (Random Forests, SVMs, KNN, Logistic Regression).

Super easy APIs for classification, regression, clustering, and dimensionality reduction.

Built-in support for data preprocessing and model evaluation.

If your project doesn't involve complex deep learning (like simple classification or regression problems), Scikit-learn is unbeatable.

It's like the old reliable pickup truck — not flashy, but it'll get you through any storm.

Hugging Face: The People's Champion

If you've been anywhere near AI in the last two years, you've heard whispers (or screams) about Hugging Face.

They provide:

Pre-trained models (especially Transformers for NLP tasks).

An easy-to-use library (transformers) that lets you fine-tune large models without selling your soul.

A thriving community and model-sharing hub.

Thanks to Hugging Face, you can literally spin up GPT-like models, BERT models, and image generation models in a few lines of code.

Bonus:

They're adding multimodal AI (text, images, audio) — making them the Avengers of AI right now.

Hugging Face feels less like a company and more like a movement. And I am proudly riding that train.

JAX: The Nerd's Dream

For the hardcore math geeks (you know who you are), there's JAX.

Developed by Google, JAX:

Makes it super easy to write high-performance mathematical code.

Specializes in autograd (automatic differentiation) and GPU/TPU acceleration.

Feels like NumPy, but supercharged.

If you want maximum control and maximum speed (but maybe fewer friends), JAX is incredible.

It's like driving a Formula 1 car — insanely powerful, but don't sneeze while steering.

Which Framework Should You Choose?

Quick cheat sheet:

Beginner or Prototyping Fast? -> **Keras**

Building Research Models or Flexibility? -> **PyTorch**

Production Deployment at Scale? -> **TensorFlow**

Classic ML without Deep Learning? -> **Scikit-learn**

Pretrained NLP and Vision Models? -> **Hugging Face**

Hardcore Math Wizards? -> **JAX**

Honestly, there's no "one-size-fits-all" — real pros often mix and match depending on the project.

It's like choosing between pizza, tacos, and sushi. Sometimes, you just get all three.

Final Thoughts (and a Shameless Metaphor)

Choosing your ML framework is like picking your battle weapon in a fantasy game.

Want a magic staff? A laser sword? A tactical rubber chicken?

Each tool gives you power — but it's how you use it that wins the quest.

In the next chapters, we'll finally build and run real generative models, so sharpen your swords (and upgrade your Python), because things are about to get even cooler.

See you on the battlefield, fellow AI warrior.

Chapter 4: Building Blocks of Generative Models

Alright, now that you know how the kitchen works, it's time to look inside the pantry. What exactly are these models made of? Probability? Vibes? Witchcraft? Not quite—but you're not too far off. This chapter is about the fundamental ingredients behind the AI magic that makes your text look poetic and your selfies look like Renaissance paintings.

Here, we dig into the core mathematical and conceptual components behind generative models. Topics include probability distributions, sampling techniques, latent spaces, and the difference between training and inference. You'll also learn about the loss functions that drive learning and the evaluation metrics that help us measure success in creative AI tasks.

4.1 Probability Distributions and Sampling

When I first started learning about probability distributions, I thought, "Great. Math. Again."

And when I heard about sampling, I assumed it meant grabbing free snacks at a grocery store.

Spoiler: it's not snacks (sadly), but it's still pretty essential if you ever want to build a generative model that doesn't behave like a confused squirrel.

Let's break down what distributions and sampling actually mean — in a way that won't give you high school math flashbacks.

What is a Probability Distribution?

Imagine you have a bag full of different colored marbles. If you reach in and pull one out, the color you get isn't guaranteed — it's based on chance.

That "chance map" — the list of how likely you are to pick each color — is basically a probability distribution.

In AI and machine learning, probability distributions are how we describe randomness and uncertainty.

In fancy terms:

A probability distribution assigns a likelihood (a number between 0 and 1) to each possible outcome.

In human terms:

It's how we tell a model, "Hey buddy, some things happen a lot, some things barely happen at all, and here's how you should guess."

Common Types of Distributions You'll Bump Into

There are lots of distributions out there — each useful depending on what you're modeling. Here are a few celebrity guests you should know:

Uniform Distribution

Every outcome is equally likely. Like rolling a fair die — every side has the same chance.

Normal Distribution (aka the Bell Curve)

Super famous. Most values cluster around the center (mean) and fewer as you move outward. Think human heights or SAT scores.

Bernoulli Distribution

Two possible outcomes: success or failure.

Like flipping a coin (heads or tails) or getting a text back (haha, just kidding, it's always "seen").

Categorical Distribution

Picking one outcome from multiple classes.

Great for things like, "Is this photo a cat, dog, or suspiciously large rabbit?"

Multivariate Normal Distribution

Like normal distribution, but across multiple dimensions. Think of a blob instead of a bell curve.

There are tons more, but don't worry — we'll use these the most in Generative AI.

Why Distributions Matter in Generative AI

Generative AI models need to make decisions — and they can't just pull numbers out of thin air (well, they can, but it'd be chaos).

Instead, they sample from distributions to:

Pick the next word in a sentence.

Choose the next pixel in an image.

Decide how much noise to add or remove during generation.

Without distributions, AI would be like a kid playing Mad Libs while blindfolded: unpredictable, messy, and occasionally hilarious for all the wrong reasons.

When you train a model, you're often helping it learn the shape of a probability distribution that matches your data.

When you generate stuff, you're sampling from that learned distribution.

What the Heck is Sampling?

Okay, so we have a beautiful, majestic distribution. How do we actually use it to pick something?

That's where sampling comes in.

Sampling is the process of drawing a random example based on the probabilities defined by your distribution.

Example:

If a model has a 90% chance of saying "hello" and a 10% chance of saying "hey," sampling decides whether this particular run spits out "hello" or "hey."

It's a controlled randomness.

Structured chaos.

The caffeine that fuels creative AI.

Different Ways to Sample

Not all sampling is created equal. Some methods are crazier than others:

Random Sampling

Straight up: pick based on the probability.

Greedy Sampling

- Always pick the most likely option (highest probability).
- Boring but safe. Like ordering the same cheeseburger every time.

Top-k Sampling

- Cut down to the top-k most likely options, and randomly pick among those.
- It's like only choosing from the best 5 songs on an album.

Top-p Sampling (Nucleus Sampling)

- Pick from the smallest set of outcomes that together add up to p% total probability (like 90%).
- Smarter, more flexible, and very popular in language models.

Temperature Sampling

Not a full sampling strategy, but an adjustment — if you lower the temperature, the model becomes conservative; raise the temperature, and it gets more random and wild.

Low temp = boring.

High temp = your AI starts writing surreal poetry about ducks.

Visualize It: The Party Analogy

Imagine a party (pre-AI apocalypse).

A Uniform Distribution party: Everyone gets exactly the same snack.

A Normal Distribution party: Most people get pizza; a few weirdoes get tofu burgers.

Sampling is you walking around, grabbing a snack at random, based on what's popular.

If you only grab the most common snack every time (greedy sampling), you end up with a plate full of boring pizza.

If you sample more freely (high temp, top-p), you might discover the weirdly delicious caramel popcorn in the corner.

That's generative AI in action.

Why You Should Care About This

In Generative AI, how you sample can radically change what your models produce.

Text generation:

Sampling controls whether you get polite conversations or trippy dream monologues.

Image generation:

Sampling decides if your AI draws a realistic cat or some Lovecraftian horror hybrid.

Audio/music generation:

Sampling can push a model to either play Beethoven… or start free-styling jazz about pineapples.

If you don't understand distributions and sampling, you're flying blind — and your models will be just as confused as you are.

Final Thoughts (and Snack Time)

Distributions and sampling are the secret sauce of Generative AI.

Without them, your models are like confused toddlers tossing Legos everywhere.

With them, your models become master builders — stacking ideas, pixels, and sounds into something that almost feels... well, human.

Also, now that I've said the word "snacks" fifty times, I'm officially starving.

If nobody brings me caramel popcorn soon, I'm going to start sampling from the fridge like an AI with a very badly trained model.

Up next: we'll dive into the wonderful and mysterious world of Latent Spaces and Representations — trust me, it's cooler than it sounds.

Let's keep going.

4.2 Latent Spaces and Representations

Okay, confession time: the first time someone told me about "latent spaces," I thought it sounded like the name of a moody indie rock band.

"Now performing their hit single, 'Compressed Dimensions of Love' — it's Latent Space!"

Sadly (or happily?), latent spaces are actually much cooler — and way more important — especially when it comes to understanding how Generative AI actually creates things from scratch.

Today, we're going to stroll through the invisible world where AI dreams are made.

Bring your curiosity — and maybe a flashlight.

So... What is a Latent Space?

Imagine you have a messy garage. Bikes, holiday decorations, and old gym equipment are all jammed together in chaos.

Now imagine you magically compress all that stuff into neat little boxes, labeled perfectly so you can pull out anything you need instantly.

That neat, compressed, organized version of your messy garage?

That's your latent space.

In more technical terms:

A latent space is a compressed, hidden representation of your original data.

It captures the essential features and relationships without needing every messy detail.

Instead of operating directly on big, complex data (like high-resolution images or massive chunks of text), generative models often operate in a lower-dimensional, smarter space where everything important is boiled down and easy to manipulate.

In human-speak:

Latent space is like the spark notes version of your data — still full of meaning, but way easier to work with.

Why Do We Need Latent Spaces?

Simple: Efficiency. Creativity. Control.

Efficiency

Compressing data lets models process, generate, and learn faster without drowning in unneeded details.

Creativity

Latent spaces allow models to explore "in-between" ideas — combining features in new ways.

Control

We can manipulate points in latent space to tweak outputs — like moving a slider from "happy face" to "angry face" when generating images.

Without latent spaces, generative AI would be like trying to sculpt a statue using an elephant and a fire hose instead of fine chisels.

How Models Learn Latent Spaces

Generative models like autoencoders, VAEs, and even GANs often work like this:

Encoder

Takes input data (like an image) and compresses it into a smaller, denser latent representation — a vector of numbers capturing the important stuff.

Latent Space

This compressed vector floats around in a magical hidden world. Nearby points represent similar inputs.

Decoder

Takes that compact latent representation and rebuilds the original data — or creates something brand new by tweaking it!

It's like squishing a 3D sculpture into a tiny marble — and then using that marble to either recreate the sculpture or make a brand-new one.

Pretty magical, right?

What's Inside a Latent Space?

In an ideal world, a well-organized latent space contains:

Clusters of similar things

(All the cat images over here, all the dog images over there.)

Meaningful directions

(Move right? Images get older. Move left? Images get younger.)

Smoothness

Small moves in latent space lead to small, logical changes in output. No sudden jumps from "cat" to "banana," hopefully.

Fun Fact:

In some models, you can literally walk through the latent space by interpolating between points — making smooth transitions between, say, a smiling woman and a serious man. It's like playing "morphing face" magic tricks!

Latent Spaces in Different Models

Here's where you've probably seen or felt latent spaces in action:

Autoencoders

Encode inputs into latent vectors and decode back into reconstructions.

VAEs (Variational Autoencoders)

Not just learn a latent vector, but learn a distribution over the latent space — allowing sampling and variation.

GANs (Generative Adversarial Networks)

Start from random noise in latent space and turn it into realistic outputs.

Transformers (like GPT models)

Technically operate in embedding spaces — close cousins to latent spaces — where the meaning of words, sentences, and even entire paragraphs are captured compactly.

In every case, these spaces are where the model dreams, connects, and creates behind the scenes.

How We Use Latent Spaces in Practice

Latent spaces aren't just for nerdy research papers. They have practical superpowers too:

Sampling new data

Wander through latent space, pick a point, decode it — boom, new image, new song, new text.

Style transfer

Mix and match styles by blending latent representations.

Editing

Move along specific directions to modify generated content (smile more, wear glasses, change background).

Interpolation

Create smooth transitions between two different images or texts by blending their latent representations.

The possibilities are endless, like drawing squiggly paths through a universe of ideas.

Latent Spaces are Weird (But in a Good Way)

Not everything about latent spaces is sunshine and rainbows.
Sometimes:

Spaces get tangled or "folded" weirdly.

Gaps exist where no meaningful data lives.

Some regions generate complete nonsense (like trying to make an AI paint a dog but it outputs a scrambled omelet instead).

But hey — the weirdness is part of the magic.

Latent spaces are like dream worlds — not everything makes perfect sense, but the best stuff often comes from a little chaos.

Wrapping it Up (and Breaking Reality)

In short, latent spaces and representations are the invisible foundations of Generative AI.

They are how models compress, understand, and create without needing an infinite amount of memory (or patience).

Without latent spaces, generating anything meaningful would be like trying to write a novel by gluing together individual letters randomly.

With them, AI can weave complex, beautiful creations from thin air — faster, better, and sometimes weirder than you can imagine.

And hey — next time someone says "latent space" in a meeting, you can just nod wisely and say,

"Ah yes, the compressed manifold of learned representations! Quite elegant, truly."

Then immediately reward yourself with a donut. You've earned it.

4.3 Loss Functions in Generative Models

Alright, let's talk about loss functions. Now, don't roll your eyes at me just yet — I know, "Loss" sounds like something you'd experience after a Netflix binge or an embarrassing family reunion, but trust me, in Generative AI, loss functions are absolutely critical.

If you've ever tried to train a model (and even if you haven't), loss functions are like that personal trainer who yells at you to "do one more rep" and keeps track of how many push-ups you've done. They tell the model how well it's doing. "Good job! You made a realistic cat." Or, more likely, "Whoa, that's not a cat. It's an abomination."

So, grab your mental gym shorts and let's break down why loss functions are the unsung heroes of machine learning!

What's a Loss Function Anyway?

Think of a loss function as the scoreboard of a game.

It tells you how well your model is playing the game of "Generate Something Awesome."

It measures how close the generated output is to the ideal output (which we wish we could get on the first try, but alas…).

A good loss function helps the model make progress by telling it how much it messed up, while a bad loss function is like giving your model a participation trophy — it doesn't help it improve much at all.

Let's say we're training a model to generate images of dogs.

If the model generates a real dog, the loss is small (like a good grade on your homework).

If it generates a hotdog, the loss is HUGE (and the teacher will probably send you to the principal's office).

Formal Definition (for the brave)

A loss function is a mathematical function that measures the difference between the predicted output (what the model generated) and the true output (what we actually wanted).

This difference is called the error, and the loss function tells us how large that error is.

Mathematically, it's often something like:

$L(y, y') = \| y - y' \|$

where:

y = the actual correct output

y' = the predicted output

The error (or loss) is measured as the difference between these values.

But let's be real — you're probably more interested in what the loss function actually does rather than getting lost in equations.

Types of Loss Functions

Loss functions come in all shapes and sizes, and the type of problem you're solving determines which one is most appropriate. Let's explore some common types that your generative models might use:

1. Mean Squared Error (MSE)

What it is: A classic. This function measures the average squared difference between the predicted and actual values. It's like finding the "distance" between what you got and what you wanted, and then saying, "Ugh, you were that far off?"

Use case: Commonly used for tasks where the output is continuous. For example, generating numerical data or fitting a line to data.

Why it's good: It penalizes large errors big time. But it can also be sensitive to outliers (so if you mess up royally, MSE will let you know in a big way).

2. Binary Cross-Entropy (BCE)

What it is: BCE is all about binary classification — predicting something that has two outcomes (like yes/no, true/false, or dog/hotdog). It measures how well the model classifies the two possibilities.

Use case: Used for classification tasks, especially when there are only two options.

Why it's good: It works wonders for models that need to distinguish between two classes and gives a smooth gradient for learning.

Fun Fact: You might recognize BCE when your model tries to figure out whether an image is a cat or not — cats vs. not-cats. It loves those yes/no questions.

3. Categorical Cross-Entropy

What it is: Imagine you're classifying data into more than two classes — dogs, cats, birds, horses, etc. Categorical cross-entropy compares the predicted probabilities for each class and the actual class, telling you how far off your model was.

Use case: Ideal for multi-class classification tasks (like deciding if a given image is of a cat, dog, or something else entirely).

Why it's good: Works well when there are multiple possible outcomes, and it's the go-to for tasks like image classification, language generation, and more.

4. Wasserstein Loss (aka Earth Mover's Distance)

What it is: Sounds fancy, doesn't it? This is the loss function your model uses if it's trying to figure out how one probability distribution "flows" to another — basically, how to move stuff from one place to another in the most efficient way possible.

Use case: A favorite in Generative Adversarial Networks (GANs), especially the WGANs. It measures how much work it would take to turn one distribution into another.

Why it's good: It helps generate smoother, more realistic outputs in GANs by ensuring that generated samples closely match real-world data.

5. Perceptual Loss

What it is: Perceptual loss is all about quality over quantity. It doesn't just measure pixel-wise differences. Instead, it compares high-level features in the image (the ones humans care about).

Use case: Used in tasks like super-resolution (making a blurry image sharp) and style transfer (transferring artistic style to an image).

Why it's good: It's super helpful for tasks that require high-quality outputs, like images that look good to the human eye (not just mathematically accurate).

Why Does Loss Matter So Much?

Loss is like the GPS for your model's training journey. It's how the model knows whether it's heading in the right direction or about to make a wrong turn into "Oops-ville" (like that one time I tried to bake cookies without reading the recipe).

If your model's loss function is bad, your model's learning will be a mess — like trying to play chess without knowing the rules. The model will have no idea how to improve, and that means you're stuck.

Pro Tip: It's important to pick a loss function that makes sense for your model's goals. The wrong loss function can make your model as effective as a paperweight.

Loss in Action: Training a Generative Model

Alright, let's wrap it up by diving into how loss functions apply to generative models. Here's the deal:

Generative models (like GANs or VAEs) use loss to learn how to generate things that look like real-world data.

In GANs, the generator creates stuff, and the discriminator tells it whether it's real or fake. The generator's goal is to minimize its loss by fooling the discriminator.

In VAEs, the loss function ensures that the model learns to recreate the input while keeping things close to the underlying latent distribution.

Loss drives progress: The better the loss function, the better your generative model can produce realistic images, text, or sound. It's like a personal trainer for AI — it pushes the model to get better every step of the way.

Wrapping Up: Keep Your Loss in Check!

In summary, loss functions are the backbone of how generative models learn. Without them, these models would be like artists without any feedback. You know, the ones who spend hours painting... and then stare at the canvas wondering why the dog looks like a mashed potato.

So, next time your model produces something truly bizarre, just remember: it's probably not the model's fault. Check the loss function! If the model's still messing up, it could be time to try a new loss function, like trying a new diet to get rid of that extra baggage.

Stay tuned for more juicy AI goodness in this chapter, because the next stop is training vs. inference, and I promise it's just as thrilling. Or maybe it's thrilling in a totally different way. Let's see!

4.4 Training vs Inference in Generative AI

Alright, brace yourself because we're about to dive into a topic that can get a bit tricky. But don't worry, we'll keep it light and fun!

Today's focus: Training vs Inference. Sounds like a classic case of "before vs. after," doesn't it? Like baking a cake (training) and then eating it (inference). We all love the eating part, but let's be real — the baking is what gets us there.

In the world of Generative AI, training is when your model is learning, experimenting, and making mistakes — kind of like a toddler trying to walk. Inference is when it's finally ready to show off what it's learned, like that toddler confidently walking across the room… without falling.

Let's break down the whole process so you can sound like an expert at your next AI conference. Or, you know, at dinner with your friends.

What is Training?

Training is like sending your model to school. It's where all the magic happens — the hours of studying, the late-night cram sessions (well, okay, not that dramatic, but you get the point). During training, the model is learning from a massive dataset, adjusting its internal weights and parameters to make sense of the world. Basically, it's gathering all the wisdom and knowledge it can to be useful later.

How Training Works:

When a model is in training, it's trying to minimize the loss function, which we talked about earlier. It learns by adjusting its internal parameters, making small changes based on the feedback it gets (like a kid learning how to draw a straight line after several attempts). Here's a super basic breakdown:

Feed it data: The model is given input (e.g., an image, a piece of text, whatever it's designed to work with).

It makes a prediction: The model generates an output based on its current knowledge (which is pretty weak at first).

Calculate the loss: The loss function checks how far off the model's output is from the expected result.

Adjust: Based on the loss, the model adjusts its internal parameters (like changing the course when you're lost while driving).

Repeat: The process repeats over and over again, constantly adjusting until the model becomes better at its task.

Why It's Important:

Training is where the hard work happens. If the model isn't trained well, it will have a tough time generating useful outputs. Think of it like baking a cake — if you don't mix the ingredients properly, you end up with something that's not even close to edible (nobody wants a flat, burnt cake).

That's why training a generative model takes time, a good dataset, and tons of computational power. It's all about learning from mistakes until the model can start generating useful, accurate results.

What is Inference?

Now, onto the fun part: Inference! This is when the model has finished its training, and it's ready to actually do something useful. It's like the model's graduation day — it's been to school, learned its lessons, and now it gets to show off everything it's learned. Inference is when the trained model generates outputs based on new input data it hasn't seen before.

Think of it like this: You trained a model to generate realistic images of cats. During training, it learned everything it could about cats (textures, shapes, colors, and all that good stuff). Now that it's done with training, you give it a random input (maybe just some noise or a description), and boom — it generates a brand-new, never-seen-before image of a cat.

How Inference Works:

Feed it input: You provide the trained model with new data (like a prompt, a starting image, or whatever it needs to generate something).

No more learning: At this point, the model isn't learning anymore. It's simply using everything it learned during training to make a prediction.

Generate output: Based on what it has learned, the model generates an output — an image, a sentence, a song, whatever your generative AI model was designed to create.

Why It's Important:

Inference is where the real magic happens! It's the moment when your model finally puts all that training to use. No more adjustments, no more learning — it's all about using what the model knows to generate something useful. This is when your AI starts earning its keep, making those sweet, sweet predictions or outputs that we love so much.

So if training is the "learning" phase, inference is the "do something cool" phase. And, let's be real, inference is where the fun happens — generating text, creating art, or whatever wild idea your model is set up for. That's where all the excitement kicks in. The model isn't just memorizing anymore; it's creating real things.

The Key Differences Between Training and Inference

Training and inference are like two very different stages in the life of a model. Sure, they're both important, but they couldn't be more different. Here's how they stack up:

Feature	Training	Inference
Purpose	Teach the model to learn and improve	Use the trained model to generate outputs
Data	Uses labeled data (input + output)	Uses unlabeled, new input data
Computation	Intensive, requires a lot of resources	Efficient, less resource-heavy
Model Adjustment	Adjusts weights and parameters based on feedback	No adjustments, just generation
Time	Takes longer (hours, days, weeks)	Happens quickly (seconds to minutes)

As you can see, training is a lot more resource-heavy and time-consuming, while inference is when things happen quickly and efficiently.

Why Does This Matter?

So why should you care about the difference? Well, understanding training vs. inference is essential for managing the life cycle of your AI projects. Training is where you get to fine-tune the model, experiment with different datasets, and, yes, deal with those pesky overfitting and underfitting problems. Inference, on the other hand, is where you put the model to work and let it generate the cool stuff (or solve your specific problem).

Also, let's not forget the computational cost. Training is resource-intensive — you need powerful GPUs, massive amounts of memory, and a lot of time. But inference? You can run that on a much smaller machine, as long as the model's already trained. It's like having your own personal artist (in the form of a trained AI) ready to work for you!

Wrapping It Up: Training Makes Perfect, Inference Makes Magic

To wrap things up:

Training is where the magic happens behind the scenes. It's the gritty work that transforms your model from clueless to capable. Inference is when the model shows off its skills, generating results that are usable, useful, and downright impressive.

And while training is like that long, sweat-drenched workout in the gym, inference is the moment when you walk into a room and show off your toned, AI-powered muscles. Or maybe that's just me after I've spent too long in the AI world — you get the picture!

Next time you train a model, just remember: Training's the grind, inference is the glory. And if you can master both, your AI will be one powerhouse of creativity. Go ahead, make some magic.

4.5 Evaluation Metrics for Generative Tasks

Alright, let's talk about a topic that every AI enthusiast secretly dreads but absolutely needs to understand: evaluation metrics. Sounds thrilling, right? Well, if you're thinking, "Hey, this is going to be as exciting as watching paint dry," just hang tight — I promise you, evaluation metrics are far from boring once you get the hang of them.

Imagine you've just trained your generative model to generate the most photorealistic images of dogs ever. You've fed it millions of dog pictures, and now, it's time to see if your model can make a dog image that's worthy of being shown to the internet (because let's face it, the internet has standards).

But how do you measure if the model's doing a good job? Is it a good dog picture, or is it a "what on earth is that" moment? Here's where evaluation metrics come in!

Just like when you're scoring a cake at a bake-off (yes, this is the third time I've compared AI to baking — deal with it), evaluation metrics help you judge how well your model is performing. And trust me, in the world of generative AI, you need these metrics — they're the only thing standing between you and a bunch of weird, unappetizing AI-generated disasters.

Why Are Evaluation Metrics So Important?

Generative tasks in AI aren't just about generating content; they're about generating good content. Whether it's images, text, or music, your model needs to create things that humans will look at and go, "Wow, that's amazing!" (or at least "Hmm, that's pretty good").

But how do we know if the AI is actually doing well? How do we determine if it's generating something that's closer to the real deal (whether it's an image, a sentence, or anything else)? Well, this is where evaluation metrics step in.

Think about it like this: If you're baking a cake, you don't just look at it and say, "Well, I think it's fine." You cut it open (not literally in AI's case, though), taste it, and maybe even compare it to the recipe. Evaluation metrics help us do that for generative models. They allow us to compare the outputs of the model against what we'd expect as a realistic, coherent, and useful result.

Let's go over a few key evaluation metrics, and I'll keep it casual and light. Ready? Here we go.

1. Inception Score (IS)

Now, let's kick it off with one of the classic metrics: Inception Score (IS). This one is widely used for image generation tasks, especially with Generative Adversarial Networks (GANs).

What is it?

Inception Score measures both the quality and diversity of generated images. In simple terms, it checks if the generated images are realistic and varied. You don't want your model generating the same boring image of a dog over and over. The Inception Score rewards models that can create a wide variety of distinct images while still keeping them realistic.

How it works:

The model is evaluated based on how confident a pre-trained Inception Network is in classifying the generated images into distinct categories.

If the generated images look clear and realistic, and they cover many diverse categories, the score is higher.

Why it's good:

It's simple, but it works. You'll know immediately if your generated images are realistic and diverse enough. If you want your AI to generate images of a variety of cats (like a fluffy Persian, a tabby, and a sphynx), this metric will let you know how well it's doing.

2. Frechet Inception Distance (FID)

Now, if Inception Score sounds too basic for you (you overachiever, you), let's move on to something a bit more sophisticated: Frechet Inception Distance (FID).

What is it?

FID measures the distance between the distribution of features of real images and generated images in the feature space of the Inception network. Essentially, it compares how far apart the two sets of images are in terms of their visual properties.

How it works:

The model's generated images are passed through the Inception network.

The Inception network transforms both real and generated images into a feature vector (kind of like a numeric representation of the image).

The FID score calculates the difference between the real and generated feature distributions using a statistical measure called the Frechet Distance.

Why it's good:

It's a more nuanced evaluation than Inception Score and is generally considered to be a better measure of image quality. The lower the FID score, the closer your generated images are to real ones. It's like that friend who keeps pointing out the flaws in your artwork but actually helps you improve (sometimes).

3. Structural Similarity Index (SSIM)

SSIM is like the best friend of image quality metrics. It's the camera lens through which you judge the quality of an image in terms of its structural content, luminance, and texture. So, if you've ever wondered how similar your generated image is to the original (without diving too deep into pixels), SSIM has your back.

What is it?

SSIM measures the perceptual quality of an image. It compares luminance, texture, and structure between the original and the generated image.

How it works:

It compares local patterns of pixel intensities in a way that is more aligned with human perception than just measuring pixel-wise differences.

A high SSIM score indicates that the image is visually similar to the real one, while a low SSIM score indicates the opposite.

Why it's good:

It's excellent for evaluating image fidelity. If you're working on tasks like image denoising, super-resolution, or style transfer, SSIM will help you gauge if the model's outputs retain important structural information.

4. BLEU Score (for Text)

You didn't think we'd leave out text, did you? For all you natural language processing fans, BLEU Score is the go-to metric for evaluating text generation models, especially for translation tasks.

What is it?

The Bilingual Evaluation Understudy (BLEU) score measures how many n-grams (chunks of text) in the generated text match n-grams in the reference text. It's like checking how similar a generated sentence is to an ideal translation.

How it works:

The model's output is compared to a set of reference texts (like human translations or ideal outputs).

BLEU checks if the generated text matches the reference text at the n-gram level (unigrams, bigrams, trigrams, etc.).

The score is between 0 and 1, with 1 being perfect similarity.

Why it's good:

BLEU is widely used in machine translation because it focuses on matching content rather than syntax or structure. It's straightforward and reliable for text-based generative tasks.

5. Perplexity (for Text)

Let's round things out with Perplexity, the metric that gives us a quick peek into how well a language model is doing.

What is it?

Perplexity measures how well a probability model predicts a sample. In other words, it's how surprised the model is when trying to predict the next word in a sentence. A lower perplexity indicates a better model that can predict words with more confidence.

Why it's good:

For text generation tasks, a low perplexity means your model is doing a good job of producing coherent and fluent sentences. You can think of it as how confident your model is at making accurate predictions — and confidence is key.

Wrapping Up: The Numbers Don't Lie!

Alright, there you have it! A whirlwind tour of the key evaluation metrics for generative tasks. These metrics are your trusty guides to ensuring that your generative model isn't just producing random, useless content but is actually generating valuable, quality output.

In the end, remember: without evaluation metrics, you might as well be flying blind. Sure, your model might seem like it's making cool things, but how do you really know if it's any good? That's where these metrics come in.

Next time your model generates something, you'll be armed with the tools to judge it properly. So go ahead, run those evaluations, and let your model show off its skills — just make sure it's doing it well!

Chapter 5: Popular Generative Architectures

Every superhero has an origin story, and every generative model has its architecture. Some of them are elegant, some are weird, and one of them (looking at you, GANs) is basically a high-stakes cage match between two neural networks. This chapter is your guided tour of the AI Hall of Fame.

We'll explore the most influential generative architectures in use today. You'll learn how autoencoders and their cooler cousin, the variational autoencoder (VAE), work under the hood. We'll break down Generative Adversarial Networks (GANs), transformer models like GPT and BERT, and the latest crowd favorite—diffusion models. You'll gain a high-level understanding of how each functions and where they shine.

5.1 Autoencoders Explained

Alright, let's talk about autoencoders. I know, I know. You're thinking, "Oh great, another fancy term to throw into the AI soup," but don't worry, I've got your back! I promise you, autoencoders are not as complicated as they sound — in fact, they're kinda like the cool, mysterious friend in the AI world that quietly gets the job done. It's a bit like that one person who's a wizard with a Rubik's cube — not flashy, but incredibly effective.

Autoencoders are unsupervised neural networks that learn to compress data into a smaller representation (that's the encoding) and then reconstruct it back to its original form (that's the decoding). Think of it like this: Imagine you've got a giant book (a data set) and you want to make a condensed version of it that still captures all the important chapters (that's the encoding). Then, you want to reconstruct that book (or a summary) into something that resembles the original, but without all the fluff (that's the decoding).

It's like summarizing a novel, but instead of using a human to do the summarizing, you use a neural network. That's what an autoencoder does — it's like the data compression expert of the AI world. And just like every expert, it gets better with practice. But you're probably asking, "Why do we need it?" Well, buckle up because this is where things get interesting.

The Autoencoder Architecture

Let's break down how an autoencoder works, because it's not just a random process of shrinking and expanding data. There's a bit of structure here, and trust me, once you see how it fits together, it's all going to make perfect sense.

1. The Encoder:

Think of this as the data shrinker. The encoder is the first part of the autoencoder, and it's responsible for taking the original data (whether that's an image, text, or whatever data you're working with) and compressing it into a latent representation (sometimes called a code or embedding). It's like the model's way of saying, "I see all this complexity, but let's make it simpler so I can understand it better."

For example, if you give the model a picture of a dog, the encoder will take that image and distill it into a much smaller version, keeping only the most essential features — things like the shape of the dog, the fur texture, and so on. The encoder is essentially learning the most compact, essential information in a way that preserves the core essence of the data.

2. The Latent Space:

Now, the fun part. After the encoder does its job, the data is sent into the latent space (a fancy term for the compressed data). This is the bottleneck of the entire system. It's like a tiny, condensed version of the original data. You can think of this as the "middleman" between the encoder and decoder. It's the key representation of the data that contains just enough information to recreate the original.

But here's the twist — that compressed data might look nothing like the original input. It's all abstract, packed with numbers that represent relationships, patterns, and features, but the real magic is that it still holds all the necessary details for reconstruction.

3. The Decoder:

Alright, here's where the decoder comes in. This part is responsible for taking that compressed code from the latent space and reconstructing it back into something that looks as much like the original input as possible. So, if you fed the model a picture of a dog, the decoder will take that compact representation of the dog and try to re-create it in full glory.

It's a bit like the decoder is reverse engineering what the encoder did, using only the most important features from the compressed data. It's not perfect, but the goal is for the output to be close enough to the original. Think of it like a blurry version of the original picture — you get the shape, you get the context, but maybe not the fine details like the fur texture or specific colors.

Why Autoencoders Matter

At this point, you might be wondering, "Why would I even need something that tries to recreate data?" Well, let me tell you — autoencoders are super versatile and have a wide variety of uses. Here are a few reasons why they matter:

1. Data Compression:

Autoencoders are like the compression tools of the AI world. Imagine having a huge image file that's hard to manage. The encoder can take that image, compress it into a much smaller size (while keeping the key features intact), and make storage or transfer way more efficient. It's like squishing your clothes into a tiny suitcase for a trip. You might lose a few things, but you'll still have the essentials!

2. Noise Reduction:

Autoencoders can also denoise data. Let's say you've got a picture with some random noise in it (like static in an image or a grainy sound clip). The autoencoder can learn how to compress the image, and during the decoding phase, it can remove that noise to generate a cleaner version. This is super useful in fields like medical imaging, where you need crystal-clear data.

3. Anomaly Detection:

Autoencoders are often used in anomaly detection (also called outlier detection). If you train an autoencoder on "normal" data (like images of healthy cells), it will struggle to compress data that's not normal (like images of diseased cells). This is a super useful tool in industries like security and healthcare, where detecting outliers in data can reveal important issues.

4. Dimensionality Reduction:

This is one of the classic uses of autoencoders. Imagine you have a massive dataset with hundreds or even thousands of features (like images with millions of pixels). The autoencoder will compress that data into a lower-dimensional space while still maintaining the most important information. It's like squeezing a bunch of data into a smaller space while keeping its essence — perfect for making the data easier to handle in subsequent models.

Autoencoders in Action

You might be thinking, "Okay, cool, but give me a real-world example!" Well, let's say you're training an autoencoder on a dataset of fashion images (let's pretend you're the AI's personal stylist). You train the autoencoder on thousands of pictures of shoes, bags, and clothes. The encoder will learn what makes each item distinct (e.g., the color, texture, shape) and compress that information into a latent space.

When you feed it a new picture of a shoe, the encoder will look at it, compress the relevant features, and then the decoder will re-create that shoe. If it's a high-quality model, it will produce something very close to the original — maybe even better! You can apply the same principles to other types of data, from text to sound, and it works like a charm.

Wrapping It Up

Autoencoders might sound like a complicated concept at first, but they're actually pretty cool once you get the hang of them. They're compression experts, helping us squeeze out all the essential features of data, reconstructing it, and making it more manageable in the process. Whether you're looking to reduce noise, detect anomalies, or just make your life easier by reducing the dimensions of your data, autoencoders have got your back.

The best part? They don't require labels to do their job. That's right, autoencoders can work on unlabeled data, making them an essential tool for anyone working with large, complex datasets. So, don't let their name fool you — autoencoders are some of the coolest unsupervised models in the generative AI world. Now, go ahead and start using them to compress data, denoise images, or create cool generative models that'll make everyone else go, "Whoa, how'd you do that?"

5.2 Variational Autoencoders (VAEs)

Alright, buckle up because we're about to dive into one of the coolest, most mysterious cousins in the world of autoencoders — the Variational Autoencoder, or VAE. Now, I know what you're thinking: "Wait, isn't an autoencoder enough already?" And to that, I say: "Absolutely! But you know what? Sometimes, you just need a bit more flair and creativity to tackle the wild complexities of data!" Enter VAEs, the AI equivalent of extra flavor in an already delicious recipe.

You see, standard autoencoders are great at compressing data and reconstructing it. But what if we want to generate entirely new data that's similar to the input? For example, maybe you want to create new images of cats that look like the cats in your dataset, or generate new samples of handwritten digits that look like the ones from the MNIST dataset. This is where Variational Autoencoders come in and take things up a notch. They're like regular autoencoders, but with a little sprinkle of probabilistic magic to make them more creative and flexible.

At their core, VAEs learn to represent data in a probabilistic way. Instead of simply compressing data into a fixed, deterministic code, they create a probability distribution that describes the data. It's like instead of drawing a solid blueprint, VAEs are creating a flexible blueprint that can generate different variations based on the same underlying principles. Sounds cool, right?

The VAE Architecture

Just like regular autoencoders, VAEs consist of an encoder and a decoder, but with a little twist that makes them stand out. Let's break it down step-by-step.

1. The Encoder:

The encoder in a VAE is responsible for taking in the input data (let's say, an image) and mapping it to a probabilistic distribution instead of just a fixed code. Instead of learning a single compressed representation (like the deterministic code in traditional autoencoders), the VAE encoder outputs two things:

The mean of the distribution (μ).

The standard deviation (σ) — which controls how spread out the distribution is.

Together, these two parameters form a Gaussian distribution that represents the data. The magic here is that the model doesn't just "remember" a single point in the latent space — it learns a whole distribution that describes where the data points could lie.

2. The Latent Space:

Now, the fun begins. Instead of having a single point in the latent space, we have a distribution. This means the model can sample different points from this distribution during the encoding phase. Think of it like walking through a foggy landscape, but you're not walking toward a specific destination; instead, you're sampling random locations based on the distribution, giving you a variety of possible outcomes.

This probabilistic approach gives the VAE a lot of flexibility and power. Rather than memorizing exact data points, VAEs are creating continuous, smooth variations in the latent space that can be used to generate new, realistic-looking data.

3. The Decoder:

Now, the decoder comes into play, just like in a regular autoencoder. Its job is to take the samples from the latent space and transform them back into a fully-formed data point (like an image, a piece of text, etc.). So, the decoder isn't just trying to reconstruct the original data — it's actually generating new, diverse outputs that are similar to the original input data, but not exactly the same.

It's like trying to build a new image of a cat, using the learned distribution. Because the encoder's latent space has a variety of possible points (thanks to that probabilistic magic), the decoder can generate multiple plausible images of cats, rather than just reproducing one fixed image over and over.

Why VAEs Matter

Alright, we've got the technical bits out of the way — but you're probably still wondering, "Why should I care about VAEs?" Well, here's why they matter and why you should get cozy with them:

1. Generative Capabilities:

This is the main reason why VAEs are so cool. Unlike traditional autoencoders, which just reconstruct the input, VAEs are all about creating new, similar data. Whether it's generating new images, texts, or even music, VAEs can learn the distribution of data and use it to generate samples that look like the original data but are new and unique. This makes them incredibly useful for tasks like:

Image generation (e.g., create new faces, animals, or landscapes).

Text generation (e.g., generate new paragraphs of coherent text).

Music generation (e.g., create new songs in the style of Beethoven or Taylor Swift).

So, if you're into creating new content, VAEs are your creative sidekick.

2. Smooth Interpolation:

Another superpower of VAEs is their ability to smoothly interpolate between different data points. Let's say you have a dataset of images of faces. With a regular autoencoder, you might get a compressed version of one face, but with a VAE, you can smoothly interpolate between two faces. For example, you can blend one face with another by sampling different points in the latent space. This is useful for things like image morphing or generating new variations of images that are between two existing samples.

3. Anomaly Detection:

Because VAEs learn to capture the distribution of normal data, they can also be used for anomaly detection. For example, if you train a VAE on healthy medical scans, and then feed it a scan of a diseased organ, the VAE will likely fail to reconstruct that scan accurately, because it doesn't fit the learned distribution of "normal" data. This is incredibly useful in fields like fraud detection or medical imaging, where identifying outliers is key.

4. Data Augmentation:

VAEs are awesome for data augmentation. Imagine you're working on a project where you have a limited amount of data (say, a small dataset of images). Using VAEs, you can generate additional data that looks similar to the original, helping to improve the robustness of your machine learning model. It's like having an AI-driven data factory that can produce new, realistic data on-demand.

VAEs in Action

Okay, let's look at a few examples of how VAEs are used in the real world. If you've ever seen cool AI-generated art, there's a good chance a VAE was involved. Let's say you want to generate new images of faces that don't exist, but still look totally real. By training a VAE on a dataset of human faces, the VAE can generate new faces that look realistic but don't belong to any real person. It's like a photo-realistic dream!

Another popular use case is in speech synthesis. By training a VAE on speech data, you can generate new speech samples that sound natural but aren't exactly from a particular speaker. It's like creating a virtual voice actor that can speak any line in a given style.

In the field of medicine, VAEs are used to generate synthetic medical images for training purposes, creating datasets of healthy tissue that can then be used to help spot abnormalities in real patient data.

Wrapping It Up

Variational Autoencoders are like the magic wands of generative models. They take data compression and reconstruction to the next level by learning probabilistic distributions, allowing them to generate new, similar data that is both creative and realistic. Whether you're creating new images, detecting anomalies, or boosting your data augmentation game, VAEs are incredibly powerful tools that can make your machine learning projects shine.

So, if you haven't started playing around with VAEs yet, I strongly recommend you give them a go — they'll add that extra level of sophistication and creativity to your generative AI toolkit. Just remember, VAEs are not just about memorizing data — they're about learning the underlying patterns and using those to create entirely new data that feels like it could belong in the original dataset. Go ahead, let your creativity run wild with a VAE, and create something new, cool, and unexpected!

5.3 Generative Adversarial Networks (GANs)

Ah, Generative Adversarial Networks (GANs) — the rockstars of the generative AI world. If you've heard of AI-generated images, deepfakes, or any kind of realistic synthetic media, then you've probably encountered GANs. These models don't just follow the usual pattern of AI learning; they battle each other to create the most lifelike outputs. If AI models were superheroes, GANs would be those unpredictable, rebellious ones who always get the job done with flair — or a little chaos. But hey, that's part of the charm, right?

Let's set the scene: Imagine you're an artist trying to create a masterpiece, but instead of working solo, you have a rival artist beside you, constantly trying to one-up you. Every time you paint a picture, your rival critiques it, looking for flaws. The kicker? The more your rival criticizes, the better you get at painting — and the more convincing your artwork becomes. This is exactly what happens with GANs, except instead of artists, there are two neural networks: the Generator and the Discriminator. Sounds like a rivalry, right? But it's this tension that leads to the creation of some of the most stunning AI-generated images.

The GAN Architecture: The Battle Between Generator and Discriminator

At the heart of every GAN are two networks: the Generator and the Discriminator. The Generator tries to create fake data (like an image), and the Discriminator tries to determine whether the data is real (from the training dataset) or fake (generated by the Generator). The whole system works like a game of cat and mouse, where both networks improve through their ongoing competition.

1. The Generator:

The Generator's job is to create data that looks as realistic as possible, whether it's an image, a video, or any kind of content. It starts by taking in some random noise as input and transforms that noise into a sample that mimics the real data. At first, the generated data might look like a mess of random pixels, but over time, as the Generator gets feedback from the Discriminator, it learns how to create more convincing data. It's like a toddler who starts off drawing stick figures but, with enough practice and critique, ends up painting masterpieces.

2. The Discriminator:

The Discriminator acts like a critical judge. Its job is to distinguish between real and fake data. In other words, it looks at the data it's given and decides whether it's from the actual dataset or generated by the Generator. The Discriminator isn't trying to generate data; it's only trying to criticize the Generator's attempts. It evaluates the Generator's output and provides feedback, telling the Generator how close it is to fooling the Discriminator. The more the Discriminator improves at detecting fake data, the more the Generator needs to step up its game to create better fakes.

3. The Game:

The Generator and Discriminator work against each other in what's known as a min-max game. The Generator aims to minimize the Discriminator's ability to distinguish between real and fake data (i.e., the Generator wants to fool the Discriminator). Meanwhile, the Discriminator is trying to maximize its ability to correctly classify data as real or fake. The two networks continue to train and improve together, with each pushing the other to perform better. The end result is that the Generator produces incredibly realistic data — and that's where the magic happens.

Training a GAN: The Back-and-Forth

Training GANs can be a bit tricky because of this adversarial relationship. Think of it like a two-player game where the winner isn't always obvious, and both sides need to get better to make progress. Here's how the process works, step-by-step:

Initial Phase (Generator starts weak): The Generator starts by creating random noise. The Discriminator, being well-trained on real data, can easily spot that this data is fake. But the Discriminator isn't perfect — it might make mistakes, especially in the beginning.

Feedback Loop (Generator improves): The Discriminator provides feedback to the Generator, telling it whether the data was real or fake. Over time, the Generator learns from these mistakes and starts creating slightly better versions of the data, which are harder for the Discriminator to spot.

Game of Cat-and-Mouse (the battle intensifies): As the Generator gets better, the Discriminator also improves to keep up. Eventually, the Generator becomes so good at generating realistic data that the Discriminator struggles to differentiate between the real and fake data.

Nash Equilibrium (the goal): Ideally, the training process leads to a Nash equilibrium, where the Generator is creating data so realistic that the Discriminator can no longer distinguish between real and fake data. At this point, the Generator has effectively "won," creating high-quality synthetic data that's indistinguishable from reality.

Why GANs are a Big Deal

So why are GANs such a game-changer in the world of AI? Well, they're capable of generating data that is remarkably lifelike and highly useful for a range of applications. Here are a few reasons why GANs are making waves:

1. High-Quality Image Generation:

GANs are particularly famous for their ability to generate photo-realistic images. Whether it's faces, landscapes, or objects, GANs can generate new images that look so real you'd have a hard time telling them apart from actual photos. Ever seen those "AI-generated faces" that look totally human but aren't? Yup, that's GANs working their magic.

One of the most famous examples is the This Person Does Not Exist website, which uses GANs to generate random faces that don't belong to anyone in real life. The images are so convincing that it's hard to believe they aren't real.

2. Creating Deepfakes:

A more controversial use of GANs is the generation of deepfakes — videos or images where a person's face or voice is replaced with someone else's. While deepfakes have raised ethical concerns, they showcase the power of GANs to manipulate and create highly realistic media. The technology can also be used positively in areas like film production or virtual reality, where lifelike avatars or simulations are required.

3. Data Augmentation:

In many machine learning applications, having enough data is crucial. GANs can help here by generating synthetic data to augment real datasets. For example, if you're training a model to recognize cats but only have a small dataset of images, a GAN can generate new images of cats to expand your training set. This makes the model more robust and improves its performance.

4. Art and Creativity:

GANs have also found a home in the world of art and creativity. Artists are using GANs to generate new, abstract, or surreal works of art that are created through the interplay between the Generator and the Discriminator. It's like collaborating with an AI artist who's always pushing you to think outside the box!

Real-World Applications of GANs

You may have already seen GANs in action in fields like art, entertainment, and medicine, but the potential applications of GANs go way beyond that. Here are a few more areas where GANs are having a profound impact:

Fashion: GANs are used to design new clothing and accessories by training on existing fashion datasets. They can generate new, original designs that can inspire the fashion industry.

Healthcare: GANs can be used to generate synthetic medical images, which are valuable for training AI models in medical imaging without compromising patient privacy. They can also be used for drug discovery and designing new molecules.

Virtual Reality: GANs are helping to create more realistic virtual environments, avatars, and simulations, making virtual worlds more immersive.

Robotics: GANs are being used to simulate environments for robot training. Robots can be trained in virtual environments generated by GANs before being deployed in the real world.

Wrapping It Up

Generative Adversarial Networks (GANs) are an exciting and powerful part of the generative AI toolkit. By setting up a battle between two neural networks — the Generator and the Discriminator — GANs are able to generate incredibly realistic data, from images to audio to video. This adversarial process pushes both networks to improve and evolve, creating outputs that are often indistinguishable from real-world data. Whether you're creating art, generating synthetic data, or developing deepfakes (yikes), GANs are at the forefront of innovation in generative AI.

The next time you see a lifelike AI-generated image or hear about a deepfake, you'll know exactly what's behind it — a GAN working its magic. So, whether you're looking to create jaw-dropping visuals or improve your AI's creativity, GANs are your go-to model. Get ready to unleash some seriously cool AI-powered creativity!

5.4 Transformer Architectures (GPT, BERT)

Ah, the Transformer architecture – the game-changer of the AI world. If you've been paying attention to recent advancements in natural language processing (NLP), you've undoubtedly heard the term "Transformer" thrown around like it's the next big thing. Well, spoiler alert: it is. Imagine a secret sauce that took the world of AI by storm. This architecture didn't just tweak things; it revolutionized how machines process and understand language. It's like upgrading from a tricycle to a jet plane – things just got a whole lot faster and more efficient.

At the core of Transformer-based models are attention mechanisms. This is where the magic happens. No longer do these models process text one word at a time (like traditional models), but instead, they process all the words in a sentence simultaneously and pay special attention to the most relevant ones. It's like having a superpower where you can focus on the most important details, all while ignoring the less relevant noise. And this attention mechanism is what powers some of the most popular AI models in NLP, including GPT (Generative Pre-trained Transformer) and BERT (Bidirectional Encoder Representations from Transformers). So, buckle up because we're about to dive into the details of these Transformer-based models and explore how they changed the AI landscape.

The Transformer Architecture: The Foundation of NLP Innovation

Before we dive deep into the specifics of GPT and BERT, let's get a sense of what makes the Transformer architecture so special in the first place. Originally introduced in the paper "Attention is All You Need" in 2017 by Vaswani et al., the Transformer quickly became the foundation of most modern NLP models. Unlike previous models, which relied heavily on recurrent neural networks (RNNs) or long short-term memory networks (LSTMs), the Transformer architecture works its magic through an attention mechanism that can consider all words in a sentence simultaneously, instead of processing them one-by-one.

This makes the Transformer incredibly parallelizable, meaning it can handle large datasets much more efficiently than its predecessors. The Transformer consists of two main parts:

Encoder: The encoder's job is to take the input sequence (like a sentence or paragraph) and transform it into a series of hidden representations. Each of these representations corresponds to the input but with more abstract information. These representations are then passed through multiple layers of self-attention, which helps the model focus on different parts of the input sentence depending on their relevance.

Decoder: The decoder takes the hidden representations from the encoder and generates the output sequence (e.g., translation, summary, or next word prediction). This is where the magic of language generation happens, as the model uses the encoded input to generate a meaningful output based on the task.

But what makes Transformer-based models like GPT and BERT unique is how they tweak and apply this architecture to solve different language tasks. Let's break down how GPT and BERT use the Transformer to accomplish their goals.

GPT: The Autoregressive Text Generator

The GPT (Generative Pre-trained Transformer) model, developed by OpenAI, is one of the most well-known and widely used models built on the Transformer architecture. What makes GPT particularly interesting is its autoregressive nature, meaning it generates text one word at a time, with each word being conditioned on the previous words in the sequence.

How GPT Works:

GPT is pre-trained on a massive corpus of text data before it's fine-tuned on specific tasks. The pre-training involves teaching the model to predict the next word in a sequence, given the words that came before it. For example, given the sentence "The cat sat on the ___," GPT would learn to predict the word "mat" based on the patterns it has seen in its training data. Once trained, GPT can be fine-tuned for various tasks such as text generation, summarization, translation, and more.

Here's the interesting part: GPT doesn't see the whole sentence all at once. Instead, it generates one word at a time and uses that to inform the next word. So, it's kind of like an AI that's writing a story one word at a time based on what it already knows. The model keeps building on its predictions until it's finished. This allows GPT to generate coherent and creative text that feels natural, often indistinguishable from human writing.

Applications of GPT:

Text generation: Creating stories, articles, or even poetry based on a given prompt.

Code generation: Writing programming code based on a description of the task.

Conversation: Powering chatbots and virtual assistants by generating human-like dialogue.

Summarization: Condensing long pieces of text into shorter, more digestible summaries.

GPT has been so successful that it has led to multiple versions, including the highly popular GPT-3, which is capable of performing a variety of tasks with minimal fine-tuning.

BERT: The Bidirectional Contextualizer

While GPT is all about generating text sequentially, BERT (Bidirectional Encoder Representations from Transformers) takes a different approach. BERT, developed by Google, focuses on understanding the context of words in a sentence rather than generating them. The main idea behind BERT is bidirectional context, meaning it takes into account both the words before and after any given word in a sentence.

How BERT Works:

Instead of processing text left to right or right to left, BERT looks at the entire sentence at once, considering the context from both directions. This is achieved through the bidirectional attention mechanism that allows BERT to develop a richer understanding of word meanings and relationships. For example, in the sentence "The bat flew through the cave," BERT would use the context around the word "bat" to understand whether it refers to an animal or a piece of sporting equipment.

BERT is pre-trained on two main tasks:

Masked Language Model (MLM): During training, BERT randomly masks out some words in the sentence and teaches the model to predict those missing words based on their context. This helps BERT learn the relationships between words in a sentence, enabling it to develop a deeper understanding of language.

Next Sentence Prediction (NSP): BERT is also trained to predict whether one sentence follows another in a coherent manner, which helps it grasp the flow of ideas in text.

Once pre-trained, BERT is fine-tuned on specific tasks, such as question answering, sentiment analysis, or named entity recognition. Because of its bidirectional understanding of language, BERT excels at comprehension-based tasks.

Applications of BERT:

Question answering: Answering questions by extracting relevant information from a document.

Sentiment analysis: Analyzing text to determine the sentiment (positive, negative, neutral) expressed.

Text classification: Categorizing text into predefined labels (e.g., spam detection).

Named entity recognition: Identifying specific entities like people, places, or dates in a sentence.

The Transformer Revolution: Why It's a Big Deal

Transformers like GPT and BERT have fundamentally shifted the landscape of NLP by introducing a more efficient and effective way of processing language. Their ability to learn context — whether by generating coherent text (GPT) or understanding it deeply (BERT) — has made them the backbone of state-of-the-art NLP applications today.

These models are scalable, meaning they can handle vast amounts of text and still deliver impressive results. They are also pre-trained, meaning they can be adapted to a wide range of tasks without needing to be trained from scratch every time. This has opened the door to more accessible AI models that can be fine-tuned for specific use cases, democratizing AI technology and making it more powerful for everyone.

Wrapping It Up

Transformers like GPT and BERT are at the core of modern AI's success in natural language processing. They've introduced revolutionary approaches to understanding and generating text, from autoregressive models (GPT) to bidirectional contextualization (BERT). Whether you're generating creative content, improving chatbots, or analyzing text, these models are behind much of the innovation you see in AI today. So, the next time you marvel at a chatbot's human-like responses or read an article written by AI, just remember: it's all thanks to the Transformer architecture. The revolution is just beginning, and it's a very exciting time to be in the AI field!

5.5 Diffusion Models Overview

Alright, let's dive into Diffusion Models—you might be wondering, "What are these mysterious creatures, and why are they making waves in the AI world?" Well, don't worry, because by the end of this chapter, you'll not only understand what diffusion models are, but you'll also be able to confidently talk about them at your next AI meetup. And who knows, you might even be the one to start the conversation (I'll let you take the credit). So, what exactly is a diffusion model, and why is it the latest thing in generative AI?

At first glance, diffusion models sound a bit abstract. I mean, when was the last time you heard "diffusion" outside of chemistry class, right? Well, the name might be borrowed from the natural world, but these models are designed to generate high-quality images, sounds, and other forms of data by learning from the process of gradually transforming noise into structure. If you've ever seen a picture or image slowly take shape from a cloudy mess of pixels, you've seen the concept in action. This method has recently become incredibly popular due to its impressive ability to create detailed, realistic outputs with remarkable precision. So, let's break it down and see how these models do their thing.

What Exactly is a Diffusion Model?

A diffusion model is essentially a type of generative model that works by reverse engineering noise. The idea is that it starts with a random, noisy signal (imagine static on your TV screen), and then iteratively refines this signal over time, progressively "denoising" it, until a coherent image or output emerges. The process is inspired by the concept of diffusion in physics, where particles spread out and mix over time, eventually creating an equilibrium.

In the context of diffusion models, this process is reversed. Instead of diffusion occurring over time (which we typically associate with the spread of particles or heat), it is a denoising process that takes random noise and gradually refines it into a meaningful and structured output. You can think of it as starting with complete chaos and slowly turning it into something organized—like turning a jumbled mess of colors into a beautiful landscape painting.

The model is trained in two main phases:

Forward Process (Diffusion Process): The model starts with an image and adds noise to it over many steps until the image becomes almost entirely random noise. This is the "forward" diffusion process, where the model learns how to degrade an image into pure noise.

Reverse Process (Denoising Process): After learning how images degrade, the model is then trained to reverse the process—starting from pure noise and iteratively removing the noise at each step to reconstruct the image.

This process is powerful, because the model doesn't just learn how to generate one type of image, it learns how to reverse the process of destruction, making it incredibly effective at creating realistic, high-quality images, sounds, or even 3D structures.

Why Diffusion Models Are Gaining Popularity

So why is everyone so excited about these models? Well, the results speak for themselves. Diffusion models have been shown to produce incredibly realistic images— sometimes even beating the performance of other generative models like GANs (Generative Adversarial Networks) in terms of image quality and diversity.

One key advantage of diffusion models is that they tend to be more stable than GANs, which can sometimes be tricky to train (I mean, who likes an unstable model, right?). GANs rely on a game-theory setup, where two networks—the generator and the discriminator—fight against each other. While that can lead to impressive results, it also creates a lot of room for failure, such as mode collapse (where the generator starts producing very similar outputs) or instability during training.

Diffusion models, on the other hand, don't face these issues. They don't rely on the same adversarial setup and are typically easier to train. Plus, they can generate high-quality images that are sharp, detailed, and diverse. This makes them ideal for tasks like creating realistic art, deepfakes, or even medical imaging.

Applications of Diffusion Models

You may be wondering, "Okay, these models sound cool, but what can they actually do?" Well, get ready for a list of some pretty awesome applications:

Image Generation: Just like other generative models, diffusion models can create new images from scratch. Whether it's creating artwork or designing a product prototype, these models can generate photorealistic images that look like they were created by a human.

Text-to-Image Generation: One of the more popular use cases for diffusion models is text-to-image generation. With models like Stable Diffusion, you can input a textual description, and the model will generate a corresponding image. For example, "A beautiful sunset over a snowy mountain range" could generate a stunning image that perfectly matches your prompt.

Super-Resolution: Diffusion models are also being used to enhance low-resolution images, effectively adding details and increasing sharpness. This can be incredibly useful in fields like satellite imaging or medical imaging where high clarity is crucial.

Audio Generation and Enhancement: Though primarily known for their image generation capabilities, diffusion models have also shown promise in audio applications, such as audio synthesis, speech enhancement, and even musical composition.

Inpainting and Editing: Diffusion models are adept at inpainting, where they can intelligently fill in missing parts of an image. Whether it's completing a partially cropped photo or generating plausible missing pixels, these models shine at repairing and editing images.

Diffusion vs Other Generative Models

Now, let's take a quick moment to compare diffusion models with other generative models, such as GANs and VAEs (Variational Autoencoders).

GANs (Generative Adversarial Networks) rely on two networks—the generator and the discriminator—competing against each other to improve the generated output. While GANs are known for generating high-quality images, they can be harder to train and less stable, especially when dealing with complex datasets.

VAEs (Variational Autoencoders) are great at generating data but often result in blurrier images compared to GANs and diffusion models. They are typically easier to train but tend to lack the detail and sharpness that you get with diffusion models.

Diffusion Models, in contrast, use a denoising process that's more stable during training and often produces higher-quality outputs, particularly in realism and diversity. They have a unique advantage over GANs when it comes to stability and training efficiency.

Key Takeaways

Diffusion models are a type of generative model that use a two-step process—adding noise to data and then denoising it—leading to the creation of high-quality images, sounds, or other forms of data.

They are incredibly stable compared to other models like GANs, making them a go-to choice for high-quality, realistic generation tasks.

Text-to-image generation, super-resolution, and inpainting are just a few of the amazing applications of diffusion models.

While they share some similarities with GANs and VAEs, diffusion models often outperform them in terms of image quality and training stability.

So, the next time you see a breathtaking AI-generated image or listen to AI-generated music, there's a good chance that a diffusion model is behind it. The future of generative AI is undoubtedly exciting, and these models are leading the charge in creative and realistic content generation. Pretty cool, right?

Chapter 6: Hands-On with Generative AI Tools

Here's where things go from "wow, that's cool" to "whoa, I made that?" We're diving into the toolbox and getting our hands gloriously dirty. No lab coat required—just a laptop, an internet connection, and the willingness to occasionally yell at a Jupyter notebook.

This chapter walks you through setting up your development environment using Python, Google Colab, and tools from Hugging Face. You'll get introduced to machine learning libraries like TensorFlow and PyTorch, explore the difference between using pre-trained models and training your own, and finally run your first text or image generation tasks. It's your first taste of building AI-powered magic.

6.1 Setting Up Your Python Environment

Alright, let's roll up our sleeves and dive into the practical part of getting your hands dirty with Generative AI. Trust me, the first step in this exciting journey is getting your Python environment set up. It's like preparing your kitchen before you cook a delicious meal – you've got to have the right tools and ingredients before you start cooking up some AI magic.

Now, I know what you're thinking: "Python? I already know Python, I'm basically a Python wizard." And while that's awesome (seriously, you're already ahead of the game), let me tell you that setting up your environment isn't just about knowing the language. It's about making sure everything is working smoothly so that you can unleash the full power of Generative AI without any hiccups. From installing packages to setting up libraries for AI frameworks like TensorFlow or PyTorch, the right setup makes all the difference. Plus, trust me, you'll feel like a pro once everything's up and running. So, let's get started!

Step 1: Install Python and Check Your Version

First things first—do you have Python installed? If you're unsure, don't worry, I'll walk you through it. Python is essential for almost all AI tasks, and if it's not already installed, you're about to fix that.

1.1 Download Python:

Head over to python.org and download the latest version of Python. I recommend installing Python 3.x because it's the version most commonly used for modern AI and machine learning tasks. It's like getting the latest version of a superhero movie – you don't want to be stuck watching the old one!

1.2 Install Python:

Once downloaded, run the installer. Important note: Be sure to check the box that says "Add Python to PATH" before hitting "Install." This will allow you to run Python from the command line without any issues. If you forget, you might end up like me, scratching your head trying to figure out why your command line is acting like a stubborn cat.

1.3 Verify Installation:

After installation, open up your terminal or command prompt (whichever OS you're using) and type:

python --version

If everything's set up correctly, you'll see something like this:

Python 3.x.x

Awesome! You're one step closer to your generative AI adventure.

Step 2: Install a Code Editor or IDE

You could technically write Python code in any text editor (like Notepad or TextEdit), but let's be real – we want tools that help us, not hinder us. A good IDE (Integrated Development Environment) will help with things like code auto-completion, syntax highlighting, and debugging. It's like having a personal assistant for your code.

Here are a few popular options:

VS Code: Visual Studio Code is free, lightweight, and incredibly popular in the Python community. It's like the Swiss Army knife of code editors, offering tons of extensions, including ones for Python, Jupyter notebooks, and AI libraries.

Don't forget to install the Python extension for extra awesomeness!

PyCharm: If you want something a little more heavy-duty, PyCharm is a great choice. It's more like the Ferrari of Python IDEs – powerful, fast, but requires a bit more setup.

You can grab the free community version of PyCharm from here.

Step 3: Install Virtual Environments

Alright, now we're cooking with gas! One of the key aspects of Python development is managing different dependencies. You don't want your machine getting cluttered with conflicting versions of libraries. Enter virtual environments.

A virtual environment is like having your own little sandbox where you can install libraries without messing with your main Python setup. It's the equivalent of having a dedicated space for your AI experiments, so your other projects don't get in the way.

Here's how you set one up:

3.1 Create a Virtual Environment:

In your terminal, navigate to your project folder (you can create one for this project if you don't already have it). Then run:

python -m venv myenv

This command will create a folder called myenv that contains its own Python installation. You can name the environment anything you want—"myenv" is just a placeholder.

3.2 Activate the Virtual Environment:

To use the virtual environment, you'll need to activate it:

On Windows:

myenv\Scripts\activate

On macOS/Linux:

source myenv/bin/activate

You'll know it's activated because your command line will show something like:

(myenv) $

This means your Python code will now run inside this isolated environment. Nice!

Step 4: Install Essential Libraries

Here's where the fun begins. For Generative AI, you'll need a variety of powerful libraries that are optimized for machine learning and deep learning. We're going to use pip, Python's package installer, to grab all the necessary tools.

4.1 Install TensorFlow and PyTorch:

The two major deep learning libraries you'll be using are TensorFlow and PyTorch. These frameworks are like the bread and butter of AI – you're going to use them to build models, train them, and generate cool stuff. Let's install them both:

For TensorFlow:

pip install tensorflow

For PyTorch (make sure you select the correct version based on your OS and hardware, such as CPU or GPU version):

pip install torch torchvision torchaudio

4.2 Install Other Useful Libraries:

Now let's grab a few more libraries that are commonly used in generative AI tasks:

pip install numpy matplotlib pandas scikit-learn

These libraries are essential for working with data, manipulating arrays, and creating visualizations.

Step 5: Jupyter Notebooks (Optional, but Recommended)

Jupyter notebooks are game-changers for AI development. It allows you to write code in chunks, execute them interactively, and visualize results in the same place. It's like your own little AI lab.

To install Jupyter:

pip install jupyter

Once it's installed, you can start a notebook by running:

jupyter notebook

This will open a browser window where you can start writing your AI code in a notebook-style format.

Step 6: Test Your Setup

It's time for the moment of truth! Let's test your setup by running a simple script that checks if everything is working as it should. Open up a new Python file (or a new Jupyter notebook) and write this:

```
import tensorflow as tf
import torch

print("TensorFlow version:", tf.__version__)
print("PyTorch version:", torch.__version__)
```

If you see the versions of TensorFlow and PyTorch printed out, congratulations – your environment is ready to go! You're now set up to start building Generative AI models. 🎉

Conclusion

And there you have it! You've successfully set up your Python environment for generative AI. I know it sounds like a lot of steps, but it's totally worth it. Now that everything is ready to go, you can start experimenting with the most powerful tools in AI. Whether you're generating text, images, or even music, you've got the foundation to build your very own AI creations. Get ready, because the real fun is just about to begin. Happy coding, and may the AI be with you!

6.2 Using Hugging Face and Google Colab

If you're diving into the world of Generative AI, there are a few tools you're going to want to get familiar with. Hugging Face and Google Colab are two of the most essential tools in your AI toolbox. They're like peanut butter and jelly – they just work so well together. In this section, we'll go through how to use both of these platforms to turbocharge your AI experiments and let you build some seriously cool stuff, fast. Whether you're generating text with GPT or images with Stable Diffusion, these tools are going to save you a lot of time and frustration. So, buckle up!

Now, let's start by breaking down these two platforms.

Hugging Face: The AI Hub You Didn't Know You Needed

Hugging Face has rapidly become one of the most popular platforms for machine learning enthusiasts, researchers, and developers. It's like a data-driven social media where you get to share, experiment, and train with cutting-edge AI models. You can think of it as the App Store for machine learning models. Hugging Face provides access to a large repository of pre-trained models that you can use right out of the box or fine-tune to suit your own needs. It's free, easy to use, and integrates smoothly with other libraries like TensorFlow and PyTorch. Whether you're working on NLP (Natural Language Processing) tasks or computer vision, Hugging Face has you covered.

Getting Started with Hugging Face

To get started with Hugging Face, you'll need to create an account. Don't worry, it's free and easy. Just go to huggingface.co and sign up. Once you're signed up, you'll have access to the Model Hub, where you can find thousands of pre-trained models for text, images, audio, and more. You can either use these models as-is or fine-tune them for your own specific tasks.

Installation:

Once your Hugging Face account is set up, we can install the necessary Python package to interact with their models. In your Google Colab environment, you can simply run the following code to install Hugging Face's transformers library:

!pip install transformers

Once that's done, you can begin using Hugging Face models. For example, let's say you want to use GPT-2 for text generation. Here's how you would load the pre-trained GPT-2 model and tokenizer:

from transformers import GPT2LMHeadModel, GPT2Tokenizer

```
# Load pre-trained model and tokenizer
model_name = "gpt2"
model = GPT2LMHeadModel.from_pretrained(model_name)
tokenizer = GPT2Tokenizer.from_pretrained(model_name)

# Encode input and generate output
input_text = "Once upon a time in a world full of AI..."
inputs = tokenizer.encode(input_text, return_tensors="pt")
outputs = model.generate(inputs, max_length=100, num_return_sequences=1)

# Decode and print the result
generated_text = tokenizer.decode(outputs[0], skip_special_tokens=True)
print(generated_text)
```

This simple example will generate text based on the input prompt. Hugging Face models support a wide variety of tasks, including text generation, translation, summarization, and more. Whether you're working on your next novel or need to summarize a research paper, Hugging Face has tools that can help.

Google Colab: Your Personal AI Playground

Now that you've got Hugging Face installed and ready to roll, let's talk about Google Colab – the cloud-based, no-setup-required platform that's perfect for running AI experiments. Google Colab is essentially a free Jupyter notebook environment that runs in the cloud. The best part? You get free access to GPUs and TPUs – which are the muscle behind AI training and inference. So, instead of waiting forever for your local machine to train that deep learning model, you can take advantage of Colab's fast hardware to run models like a pro.

Getting Started with Google Colab

All you need to get started is a Google account (yes, the one you probably already use for Gmail). Once you're signed in, you can visit Google Colab and start a new notebook. You'll have access to a virtual machine (VM) that's ready to go. No installation required! From there, you can write Python code in cells, execute them, and see the results immediately – it's the perfect environment for experimenting with machine learning models.

You can run your Hugging Face code directly in a Colab notebook and even access the GPU by selecting it from the Runtime > Change runtime type menu. Choose GPU or TPU from the Hardware Accelerator dropdown to supercharge your training or inference tasks.

Example: Running Hugging Face on Google Colab

Now that you've got your Colab setup and Hugging Face installed, let's run an example of text generation. Here's the same GPT-2 model we loaded earlier, but this time in Google Colab:

```
# First, install Hugging Face transformers
!pip install transformers

# Now let's import Hugging Face
from transformers import GPT2LMHeadModel, GPT2Tokenizer

# Load the model and tokenizer
model_name = "gpt2"
model = GPT2LMHeadModel.from_pretrained(model_name)
tokenizer = GPT2Tokenizer.from_pretrained(model_name)

# Define the input prompt
input_text = "In a faraway land where AI ruled the world,"

# Encode and generate text
inputs = tokenizer.encode(input_text, return_tensors="pt")
outputs = model.generate(inputs, max_length=150, num_return_sequences=1)

# Decode the output text
generated_text = tokenizer.decode(outputs[0], skip_special_tokens=True)
print(generated_text)
```

This code runs seamlessly in Google Colab with a GPU, so you can generate text, run inference, or even train models quickly without needing a fancy machine at home.

Combining Hugging Face with Google Colab

When you combine Hugging Face with Google Colab, you get an incredibly powerful and efficient platform for experimenting with and deploying AI models. This duo lets you leverage the latest in AI research without worrying about hardware limitations. With

Hugging Face's vast collection of models and Google Colab's fast processing power, you can get started on projects that would otherwise require expensive resources or advanced knowledge of cloud computing.

Why Should You Use These Together?

Speed and Efficiency: Google Colab's free access to GPUs and TPUs means that you can run intensive deep learning models in no time.

Access to State-of-the-Art Models: Hugging Face provides you with cutting-edge AI models that are ready to use. No need to start from scratch.

Free: Both Google Colab and Hugging Face's Model Hub are free to use, making them accessible to everyone – from hobbyists to professionals.

Collaboration: Google Colab makes it easy to share your notebooks and collaborate with others, whether you're working on a research paper or a personal AI project.

Conclusion

There you have it – a quick intro to using Hugging Face and Google Colab to take your Generative AI projects to the next level. With Hugging Face's pre-trained models and Google Colab's GPU-powered environment, you can experiment, build, and deploy AI models faster than ever before. Whether you're generating text, creating art, or experimenting with complex machine learning tasks, these tools are your new best friends. And the best part? You don't have to worry about setting up servers, managing GPUs, or dealing with hardware issues. So, go ahead and make some AI magic – you're just a few lines of code away from greatness! Happy coding!

6.3 Intro to TensorFlow and PyTorch

Alright, let's talk about two of the most important deep learning libraries that you'll be using on your AI journey: TensorFlow and PyTorch. If Hugging Face is your trusty AI toolbox, then TensorFlow and PyTorch are the powerful wrenches and screwdrivers inside that box. These two libraries are at the core of modern AI development, and knowing how to use them will make you feel like an AI wizard. Whether you're trying to generate some cool text, create stunning images, or dive into complex deep learning models, you're going to want to get cozy with TensorFlow and PyTorch. Don't worry – I've got your back.

Now, let's dive in, and I'll guide you through the basics of TensorFlow and PyTorch, and show you how they differ, so you can pick the best one for your specific needs.

What is TensorFlow?

TensorFlow is one of the most well-known and widely used deep learning libraries out there. Created by Google, it's an open-source framework that helps developers and researchers build AI models for everything from image recognition to natural language processing (NLP). If you're working on large-scale projects that require high-performance computation (like training on huge datasets or working with complex models), TensorFlow is often your go-to tool.

TensorFlow is designed to be highly scalable, meaning you can run your models on everything from a personal laptop to massive distributed computing systems. TensorFlow is especially popular for building production-ready models—it's got the full package, from research prototypes to deployment in real-world applications.

TensorFlow Features:

Scalability: TensorFlow can run on almost any platform, from your local machine to large-scale distributed systems.

Deployment: TensorFlow is great for turning your models into production-ready applications. With TensorFlow Lite, TensorFlow.js, and TensorFlow Serving, you can deploy models to mobile, web, or even production servers.

TensorFlow Hub: Access pre-trained models from TensorFlow Hub to save time on training.

Here's a quick example of how to use TensorFlow to build a simple neural network:

```
import tensorflow as tf
from tensorflow.keras.models import Sequential
from tensorflow.keras.layers import Dense

# Create a simple neural network
model = Sequential([
    Dense(64, activation='relu', input_shape=(10,)),
    Dense(64, activation='relu'),
```

```
    Dense(1, activation='sigmoid')
])

# Compile the model
model.compile(optimizer='adam', loss='binary_crossentropy', metrics=['accuracy'])

# Fit the model
model.fit(x_train, y_train, epochs=10, batch_size=32)
```

In this code, we're creating a simple feed-forward neural network with two hidden layers. TensorFlow's Keras API (which is included within TensorFlow) makes it incredibly easy to build and train models.

What is PyTorch?

On the other side, we have PyTorch – a deep learning library developed by Facebook's AI Research lab. PyTorch has become incredibly popular, especially in the research community, because it's known for being flexible and dynamic. Unlike TensorFlow, PyTorch allows you to build models dynamically – meaning you can modify the network architecture as you run the code. This feature is incredibly useful when you're experimenting and trying out new things.

PyTorch is also known for being Pythonic. Its syntax feels very natural, and it works well with other Python libraries. Many people find PyTorch easier to get started with, and some even argue that it has better documentation and support for debugging. So, if you're just starting with deep learning and want a smooth and intuitive experience, PyTorch might be your best bet.

PyTorch Features:

Dynamic Computational Graph: PyTorch uses dynamic computation graphs, meaning the graph is defined as the operations are executed. This makes debugging easier, as you can change the model during execution.

Tensors: PyTorch's core data structure is the Tensor, similar to NumPy arrays, but with support for GPU acceleration. This makes it easy to run computations on a GPU.

Deep Integration with Python: PyTorch feels very native to Python developers. It integrates seamlessly with Python libraries like NumPy, SciPy, and others.

Here's an example of building a neural network in PyTorch:

```
import torch
import torch.nn as nn
import torch.optim as optim

# Define a simple neural network class
class SimpleNN(nn.Module):
    def __init__(self):
        super(SimpleNN, self).__init__()
        self.fc1 = nn.Linear(10, 64)
        self.fc2 = nn.Linear(64, 64)
        self.fc3 = nn.Linear(64, 1)

    def forward(self, x):
        x = torch.relu(self.fc1(x))
        x = torch.relu(self.fc2(x))
        x = torch.sigmoid(self.fc3(x))
        return x

# Initialize the model
model = SimpleNN()

# Define loss function and optimizer
criterion = nn.BCELoss()
optimizer = optim.Adam(model.parameters(), lr=0.001)

# Training loop (simplified)
for epoch in range(10):
    optimizer.zero_grad()  # Zero out gradients
    output = model(x_train)  # Forward pass
    loss = criterion(output, y_train)  # Compute loss
    loss.backward()  # Backpropagation
    optimizer.step()  # Optimize weights
```

As you can see, the code structure in PyTorch is a bit more flexible compared to TensorFlow's Keras API, allowing you to define and manipulate the model in real-time. This flexibility is great for experimenting with different architectures or developing complex models.

TensorFlow vs. PyTorch: Which Should You Choose?

Both TensorFlow and PyTorch have their strengths, and your choice will depend on your project needs. Here's a quick comparison to help you decide which library might be best for your AI projects.

Feature	TensorFlow	PyTorch
Ease of Use	Keras API makes it user-friendly	Flexible, Pythonic, easier for research
Deployment	Excellent deployment tools (TensorFlow Lite, TensorFlow Serving)	Great for research and prototyping, but deployment tools are catching up
Community Support	Large, well-established community	Growing community, particularly in research
Dynamic vs Static Graphs	Static computation graph (easier for optimization)	Dynamic computation graph (great for experimentation)
Performance	Excellent on large-scale, production models	Often more flexible but may not scale as well in production
Debugging	Easier with TensorFlow 2.x (Eager Execution)	Very easy due to dynamic graph

When to Use TensorFlow:

When you need a scalable solution for production.

If you're building large-scale applications or models that need to be deployed (e.g., in mobile apps or cloud services).

If you're working on real-time applications where performance is key.

When to Use PyTorch:

If you're doing research or experimenting with new ideas.

When you want to easily debug or modify your models during execution.

If you prefer a Pythonic experience and find dynamic graphs more intuitive.

Conclusion

Whether you choose TensorFlow or PyTorch will depend on your needs, but you can't go wrong with either one. TensorFlow is perfect for production environments and large-scale models, while PyTorch shines in the research and development space thanks to its flexibility and ease of use. Both libraries are constantly evolving, so no matter which one you choose, you'll have access to some of the best tools available for building and deploying Generative AI models.

And here's the best part: you don't have to choose just one. You can use both in different parts of your AI pipeline. It's like choosing between a hammer and a screwdriver – both are great tools, and together, they can help you build something amazing. So, get out there, experiment, and start building some incredible Generative AI models. Happy coding!

6.4 Pre-trained Models vs Training from Scratch

Alright, so here's the deal: you're ready to dive into the exciting world of Generative AI, but there's a big decision ahead of you. Do you go the pre-trained model route or roll up your sleeves and start training from scratch? It's a bit like the age-old question: do you bake your own pizza dough or order from your favorite local pizzeria? Both options can lead to something amazing, but the right choice depends on your goals, time, and level of expertise. Don't worry though – we'll break it down so you can make the best decision for your project.

In this section, we'll take a deep dive into pre-trained models and training from scratch, looking at the pros and cons of each approach. We'll also discuss how you can make use of the ever-growing number of pre-trained models out there and when it's still beneficial (or even necessary) to start from the ground up.

Pre-trained Models: Ready to Use and Time-Saving

Let's start with the obvious: pre-trained models are like off-the-shelf solutions that have already been trained on massive datasets. They're ready to go, saving you time and computational resources. This is particularly useful when you want to dive into a project quickly without spending hours (or even days) training a model from scratch. Whether you're interested in text generation, image synthesis, or speech recognition, there are pre-trained models available that you can use right away, with little to no customization needed.

Why Use Pre-trained Models?

Time-Saving: Training a model from scratch can take days, weeks, or even longer, especially if you're working with large datasets. Pre-trained models are already optimized and fine-tuned, so you can skip the boring (and time-consuming) training process.

Lower Computational Cost: Training deep learning models requires powerful hardware (think GPUs or TPUs) that can be expensive to maintain. Pre-trained models allow you to leverage the work that's already been done by others and save on costly infrastructure.

Quality Models: Pre-trained models are often built by experts using massive, diverse datasets. You get access to cutting-edge models like GPT-3, BERT, and StyleGAN, which have been optimized for specific tasks.

Transfer Learning: You can take a pre-trained model and fine-tune it for your specific task, saving a ton of time and resources. This is called transfer learning, and it's one of the most powerful techniques in modern machine learning. Instead of training a model from scratch, you build on the knowledge it's already acquired.

Example: Fine-Tuning Pre-trained Models with Hugging Face

Let's say you're working on a text generation project using GPT-2, one of the most popular pre-trained models. Instead of training GPT-2 from scratch, you can simply fine-tune it to suit your specific needs. Here's how you could do that:

```
from transformers import GPT2LMHeadModel, GPT2Tokenizer, Trainer,
TrainingArguments

# Load pre-trained GPT-2
model = GPT2LMHeadModel.from_pretrained("gpt2")
tokenizer = GPT2Tokenizer.from_pretrained("gpt2")

# Fine-tune the model with your dataset
training_args = TrainingArguments(output_dir="./results", num_train_epochs=3)
trainer = Trainer(model=model, args=training_args, train_dataset=train_dataset)
```

trainer.train()

In this example, you're taking a pre-trained GPT-2 model and fine-tuning it with your own dataset. This saves you the trouble of starting from scratch while still allowing you to tailor the model to your specific needs.

Training from Scratch: The DIY Approach

On the flip side, there are times when training a model from scratch is the best option, particularly if you have a unique dataset or a very specific task in mind. Think of it as baking your own pizza dough — it might take longer, but the result is fully customized to your liking.

Why Train from Scratch?

Custom Datasets: If you have a unique dataset that isn't well-represented in pre-existing models, training from scratch might be your only option. Pre-trained models are great for general use cases, but they might not work well on niche tasks or specialized data.

Complete Control: When you train from scratch, you have full control over the architecture, hyperparameters, and training process. You're not limited by the design of a pre-trained model, so you can experiment and tweak things to your heart's content.

Improved Performance: In some cases, training a model from scratch can lead to better performance, especially if you have a large and well-labeled dataset. Pre-trained models may not be able to fully capture the nuances of your specific data, whereas a custom model can be fine-tuned to suit it perfectly.

Learning Opportunity: Training from scratch can be an incredible learning experience. You'll gain a deeper understanding of how neural networks work and learn to troubleshoot when things go wrong. Plus, you'll get to play with advanced techniques like backpropagation, optimizers, and gradient descent.

Example: Training a Neural Network from Scratch in PyTorch

Let's say you want to build a simple neural network from scratch in PyTorch. Here's a minimal example of how you could do that:

import torch
import torch.nn as nn

```python
import torch.optim as optim

# Define the network architecture
class SimpleNN(nn.Module):
    def __init__(self):
        super(SimpleNN, self).__init__()
        self.fc1 = nn.Linear(10, 64)
        self.fc2 = nn.Linear(64, 64)
        self.fc3 = nn.Linear(64, 1)

    def forward(self, x):
        x = torch.relu(self.fc1(x))
        x = torch.relu(self.fc2(x))
        x = torch.sigmoid(self.fc3(x))
        return x

# Initialize the model, loss function, and optimizer
model = SimpleNN()
criterion = nn.BCELoss()
optimizer = optim.Adam(model.parameters(), lr=0.001)

# Training loop (simplified)
for epoch in range(10):
    optimizer.zero_grad()  # Zero out gradients
    output = model(x_train)  # Forward pass
    loss = criterion(output, y_train)  # Compute loss
    loss.backward()  # Backpropagation
    optimizer.step()  # Optimize weights
```

In this example, we're defining a basic fully connected neural network and training it from scratch. You have total control over the entire process, from defining the layers to choosing the optimizer and loss function.

When to Choose Pre-trained Models vs Training from Scratch

Both pre-trained models and training from scratch have their time and place, so here's a handy guide to help you decide which approach is right for your project:

Choose Pre-trained Models When:

You want to get started quickly with a ready-made solution.

You're working on a project with a general task (e.g., text generation, image classification) and you don't need to customize the model too much.

You want to save time and computational resources.

You have a smaller dataset, or you want to fine-tune a model on your data.

Choose Training from Scratch When:

You have a unique dataset or a very specific task that pre-trained models don't handle well.

You want complete control over the model architecture and hyperparameters.

You're looking for maximum performance and are willing to put in the time to optimize the model.

You want to learn more about the inner workings of deep learning.

Conclusion

Ultimately, the choice between pre-trained models and training from scratch depends on your project needs, timeline, and available resources. For many projects, pre-trained models are the way to go. They save time, are cost-effective, and give you access to state-of-the-art models. But if you have a unique project or a specialized task, training from scratch can give you the freedom and flexibility you need to build something truly custom.

And remember – whether you're using a pre-trained model or building one from scratch, the world of Generative AI is your playground. So, roll up your sleeves, have fun experimenting, and don't be afraid to try both methods. There's no one-size-fits-all approach, but with a little creativity, you'll be creating AI magic in no time. Happy building!

6.5 Running Your First Text or Image Generation

Alright, the moment has arrived. You've set up your environment, learned the ins and outs of Python, and figured out what the heck is going on with those pre-trained models. Now, it's time to see the magic happen. You're about to run your first text generation or image generation model, and trust me, it's going to be an experience you'll remember—especially when the AI spits out something completely unexpected, like a talking cat or a surreal version of a famous painting. Don't worry, that's just the AI flexing its creative muscles. It's a wild ride, but it's the fun kind.

Let's walk through the process of generating both text and images with pre-trained models. Whether you're crafting a chatbot that sounds like Shakespeare or creating mind-bending art, you'll be amazed at how simple it can be to get started. By the end of this section, you'll be able to run your very own text generation or image generation model using platforms like Hugging Face, Google Colab, and the power of your own coding skills.

Running Your First Text Generation

For text generation, one of the easiest ways to get started is by using the GPT-2 model from Hugging Face. GPT-2 is a language model that can generate coherent and contextually relevant text based on an input prompt. Whether you want to write stories, generate conversational AI responses, or simply see how good GPT-2 is at pretending to be Shakespeare, this model can handle it. Let's get your first text generated!

Step 1: Install Hugging Face Transformers

First, you need to install the transformers library from Hugging Face. Open up your terminal (or a Google Colab notebook) and install the library using this command:

!pip install transformers

Once the library is installed, you'll be ready to use pre-trained models like GPT-2 for text generation.

Step 2: Import the Model and Tokenizer

Next, you'll need to load the GPT-2 model and its tokenizer. The tokenizer helps convert the text into a format that the model can understand. Here's how you load the model:

from transformers import GPT2LMHeadModel, GPT2Tokenizer

 # Load pre-trained model and tokenizer
model = GPT2LMHeadModel.from_pretrained("gpt2")

```
tokenizer = GPT2Tokenizer.from_pretrained("gpt2")
```

Step 3: Generate Text from a Prompt

Now comes the fun part! You can define a starting prompt and let GPT-2 generate some text. Here's a simple example:

```
# Define a prompt for text generation
prompt = "Once upon a time in a faraway land, there was a dragon named Ignatius who"

# Encode the prompt
inputs = tokenizer.encode(prompt, return_tensors="pt")

# Generate text
outputs = model.generate(inputs, max_length=200, num_return_sequences=1, no_repeat_ngram_size=2)

# Decode and print the output
generated_text = tokenizer.decode(outputs[0], skip_special_tokens=True)
print(generated_text)
```

What's Happening Here?

Prompt: You give the model a starting sentence or idea. GPT-2 takes it and runs with it.

Encoding: We convert the prompt into numbers that the model can understand.

Generation: GPT-2 generates new text based on the prompt. The max_length controls how long the generated text will be.

Decoding: Finally, we convert the generated numbers back into readable text.

And voilà! You'll see a story unfold before your eyes, starting from your prompt and going off into uncharted territory. Sometimes, the AI will surprise you with some truly weird and hilarious twists.

Running Your First Image Generation

Now let's move on to generating images. This is where things get really cool (and occasionally surreal). One of the best models for image generation is StyleGAN2, but if you want a simpler, more accessible approach, you can use a pre-trained Stable Diffusion model. Stable Diffusion is a generative model that creates images based on text prompts. Think of it as a text-to-image art generator that can create anything from realistic landscapes to surreal sci-fi worlds.

Step 1: Install Dependencies

First, you'll need the diffusers library from Hugging Face, which makes working with Stable Diffusion easy. Install it with the following command:

!pip install diffusers

You'll also need to install torch if you haven't already, since that's the library used to run the models:

!pip install torch

Step 2: Load Stable Diffusion

Once your environment is set up, it's time to load the Stable Diffusion model. Here's how you can do it:

from diffusers import StableDiffusionPipeline

 # Load pre-trained Stable Diffusion model
pipe = StableDiffusionPipeline.from_pretrained("CompVis/stable-diffusion-v-1-4-original")
pipe.to("cuda") # Use GPU if available for faster generation

This code loads the pre-trained Stable Diffusion model. You can specify whether you want to run it on a GPU for faster processing by using pipe.to("cuda").

Step 3: Generate Your First Image

Now, let's generate some art! You just need to provide a text prompt, and the model will generate an image based on that description. Here's an example:

 # Define a text prompt

```
prompt = "a futuristic city at sunset, with flying cars and neon lights"

# Generate an image
image = pipe(prompt).images[0]

# Display the image
image.show()
```

What's Happening Here?

Prompt: The model uses your text prompt to understand what kind of image you want. You could ask for anything, from a sunset over a forest to a robot sipping coffee in a café.

Image Generation: The model takes your prompt and creates an image from it. Depending on the complexity of the description, the result can range from something straightforward to something a little more abstract.

Display: We then display the generated image using image.show(). You can save the image or modify it further if you like.

The Surreal (and Fun) Side of Generative AI

As you start generating text and images, remember that AI is creative, but it's also quirky. You might ask for a "cat playing piano" and get a cat dressed like Mozart, or generate a "dystopian city" and end up with a neon-lit urban jungle full of bizarre, floating shapes. The beauty of generative models is that they have a mind of their own, and sometimes the results are hilarious, unexpected, or downright weird. That's part of the fun— embracing the unpredictable nature of AI!

Pro Tip: Get Creative!

The more specific and detailed your prompts, the more interesting the results will be. Try mixing concepts like "a dragon made of fire, flying through a starry sky" or "a robot painting a portrait of itself in a Victorian dress." The weirder, the better. Trust me, the AI won't judge you (but your friends might).

Conclusion

Congratulations, you've just run your first text generation and image generation models! Whether you're creating a sci-fi story or generating surreal art, the possibilities are endless with these tools. You now have the power of GPT-2 and Stable Diffusion at your fingertips to fuel your creativity. So, go ahead—get weird, get wild, and let the AI magic unfold.

Chapter 7: Generative AI for Text

Ever wanted a robot to write your emails, craft poetry, or generate fantasy lore about a squirrel uprising? Welcome to text generation, where language models take the stage—and sometimes steal the show. This chapter is all about giving AI a voice, and trust me, it has a lot to say.

We'll cover the mechanisms behind how language models generate coherent, context-aware text. Key topics include prompt engineering, text summarization, translation, and style transfer. You'll also be introduced to ethical considerations surrounding AI-generated content, including plagiarism, misinformation, and AI bias in natural language processing.

7.1 How Language Models Generate Text

Ah, the magic of language models. You know the ones—those AI systems that can churn out sentences, paragraphs, or entire stories just by reading a few words. The ability to generate text that sounds natural, coherent, and sometimes even poetic, has captured the imagination of many. But how do they do it? Are there tiny robots inside that tap away at a keyboard, or is there some deep AI wizardry going on? Spoiler alert: It's neither. Instead, it's all about mathematics, probabilities, and some seriously impressive machine learning techniques.

Now, if you've ever used a language model like GPT (Generative Pre-trained Transformer), you've probably noticed that when you type a prompt, it responds with a surprisingly relevant and articulate piece of text. The secret sauce? Language models are trained on vast amounts of text data—books, articles, websites, and more. They learn patterns, structures, and word associations to generate human-like responses to the prompts they receive. Think of it like teaching a parrot to speak: at first, it mimics words, but eventually, it gets pretty good at stringing them together to sound like it knows what it's talking about. But instead of feathers, these "parrots" have a deep neural network.

The Mechanics Behind Text Generation

To understand how these language models generate text, we need to break it down a bit. At the core, most modern language models, like GPT-3, use a type of architecture called Transformers. Transformers are essentially a series of algorithms that allow the model to handle and generate text based on the context of the words in the input. To keep it simple, imagine trying to write a sentence where every word depends on the one before it. But instead of just looking at the most recent word, Transformers have the ability to look back at the entire sentence (or even paragraph) to determine the best next word to use.

Step 1: Pretraining on Massive Text Corpora

Before a model can generate any useful text, it first needs to undergo pretraining. This process involves exposing the model to vast amounts of text data. You might think of it like feeding the model a diet of books, news articles, and social media posts—lots and lots of text, basically. During pretraining, the model doesn't learn specific tasks like answering questions or writing poems. Instead, it learns general patterns about how language works. For example, it learns things like:

Which words are most likely to come together (like "peanut butter" and "jelly").

How sentences are structured (subject, verb, object).

How to maintain coherence in longer passages of text.

By learning these patterns, the model builds an internal understanding of language that can be applied to many different tasks.

Step 2: Fine-Tuning for Specific Tasks

After the pretraining, the model can then be fine-tuned for specific tasks. Fine-tuning involves training the model on a smaller, specialized dataset that's more task-specific. This is where the model can get a little more clever. It's kind of like teaching a dog to fetch: the first part is just learning the basics, but the fine-tuning is where you get the dog to fetch the exact item you want. For a language model, fine-tuning could involve focusing on generating text for a particular domain (like medical reports, casual conversation, or even jokes).

During fine-tuning, the model learns to generate text that's not only fluent but also relevant to specific types of input. So, while GPT might start by generating random sentences, fine-tuning gives it the ability to perform useful tasks, like answering questions, completing sentences, or even writing essays based on prompts.

Step 3: The Magic of Probability

Once the model is trained, the actual process of generating text boils down to probability. When you give a language model a prompt, it essentially guesses the most likely next word based on everything it has learned. For example, if your prompt is "The sun is shining and the," the model might predict the next word is "birds" because that's a common association. But it could just as easily predict "flowers," "sky," or even "clouds," depending on what it has learned.

This is where probability distributions come into play. The model assigns a probability to each possible next word and picks the one with the highest probability. But it doesn't just pick the most probable word—it sometimes adds a bit of randomness to make the output feel less robotic. This is why AI-generated text can sometimes be quirky, or even downright hilarious, as it balances probability with a touch of creative freedom.

Step 4: Tokenization and Encoding

Before the model even begins generating text, it needs to understand the input. This is where tokenization comes in. Tokenization breaks the input text into smaller units, or tokens, that the model can process more easily. These tokens can represent words, subwords, or even characters, depending on the model's configuration. For example, the sentence "I love AI" could be split into three tokens: "I," "love," and "AI." Each of these tokens is then converted into a numerical representation (called embeddings) that the model can process. These embeddings are fed into the model, which uses them to predict the next token in the sequence.

Step 5: Decoding the Output

Once the model has generated a sequence of tokens, it needs to decode them back into human-readable text. This is where the magic happens. The model takes the numerical representations of the tokens and converts them back into words, assembling them into a coherent response. If everything goes well, you'll get a response that sounds like it came from a human (or at least from a very clever parrot with a PhD in language).

The Power of Context

One of the most remarkable things about modern language models is their ability to understand and generate contextual text. This means that the model doesn't just look at the last word you typed and guess the next one. It's constantly analyzing all the words in the prompt to figure out the bigger picture. This ability to maintain context is why GPT-3 and other transformers can generate not just grammatically correct text, but text that feels cohesive and relevant.

For example, if you ask a language model to write a story about a dragon, it will not only recall facts about dragons but also pull from its broader understanding of storytelling conventions—like how a plot typically progresses, or how dragons often get involved in epic battles. It's this ability to generate text that fits within a narrative or broader context that sets language models apart from more basic AI systems.

Wrapping It Up

So there you have it: language models generate text using a combination of pretraining, fine-tuning, probability, and some pretty sophisticated algorithms. It's a process that involves understanding language, predicting the most likely next word, and then putting it all together into something that sounds like it was written by a human (or, at least, like it makes sense). Of course, this isn't a perfect science—sometimes the AI might write something completely nonsensical, but that's part of the charm. In the world of Generative AI, every day is an adventure, and you never quite know what the model will come up with next. So, go ahead—ask it to write you a poem about an elephant in space. Who knows? You might get a masterpiece.

7.2 Prompt Engineering Basics

Let's be honest — when I first heard the term "prompt engineering," I thought it sounded like something that required a hard hat and a clipboard. Maybe even some steel-toed boots. But no, sadly (or happily, depending on your feelings about manual labor), prompt engineering is all about crafting clever, strategic ways to talk to AI models so they actually give you what you want. Think of it like ordering at a drive-thru: if you just grunt vaguely, you might end up with a fish sandwich when you really wanted a cheeseburger. Clear communication is key, even when you're dealing with a brain made of math instead of meat.

In the world of generative AI, prompt engineering is quickly becoming an essential skill. You don't just type "make art" or "write story" and expect a masterpiece. No, you gotta woo the model a little, give it the right cues, and nudge it along the right path. It's like AI dating. Be too vague and you get weird, robotic nonsense. Be too specific and you crush its creativity. But if you hit that sweet spot? Oh man, you and the AI can make magic together.

What Exactly is Prompt Engineering?

Formally speaking (because sometimes we do have to sound like grown-ups), prompt engineering is the practice of designing, structuring, and refining inputs (prompts) to elicit the best, most useful responses from a generative AI model. It's part science, part art, and part trial-and-error wizardry.

When you prompt an AI, you're basically setting the stage. You're defining:

The task you want it to perform

The style you want it to use

Any constraints or rules it should follow

Sometimes even the persona it should adopt

Think of prompts as programming commands written in plain English (or whatever language you're using). Instead of code, you're giving "natural language instructions" — but trust me, crafting them well can sometimes feel just as tricky as writing software.

The Anatomy of a Good Prompt

So, what separates a brilliant prompt from a boring one? A few key ingredients:

Clarity: Be clear about what you want. If you want a two-paragraph story about a robot pirate in Shakespearean style, say that.

Context: Set the scene. If you want the model to imagine it's a travel agent or a medieval knight, let it know upfront.

Specificity: The more specific your request, the better the AI can deliver. "Write a poem" is fine, but "Write a haiku about rain on a tin roof" will get you closer to what you envision.

Constraints: Giving limits ("Use fewer than 100 words" or "Only answer with bullet points") helps the model stay on track.

Examples: Sometimes, you can even include a few examples of what you want to really dial it in.

Good prompts can feel like you're leading the AI by the hand toward your goal without shoving it so hard that it falls over confused.

Types of Prompts You Should Know

Here are a few popular styles of prompts that can work like magic, depending on what you need:

Instructional Prompts:

"Explain how photosynthesis works in simple terms."

Creative Prompts:

"Write a sci-fi story set in a world where plants have taken over."

Role-based Prompts:

"Pretend you are a wise 15th-century monk giving advice."

Q&A Prompts:

"What are five fun facts about jellyfish?"

Comparison Prompts:

"Compare the leadership styles of Napoleon and Julius Caesar."

Chain-of-Thought Prompts:

"Step-by-step, explain how to bake a cake."

The style you choose totally depends on what you're trying to get the AI to produce. Sometimes you'll mash up a few styles into one mega-prompt, and that's perfectly okay too.

Common Mistakes (aka How to Make AI Go Weird)

Learning prompt engineering is mostly about learning from your own hilariously bad prompts. Here are some common mistakes to avoid:

Being Too Vague:

"Tell me about stuff" is gonna get you a hot mess.

Overloading the Prompt:

If you cram five separate ideas into one prompt, the AI will likely mash them up into something strange (and not the cool kind of strange).

Ignoring Context:

If you ask for a professional email but don't say who it's to or about what, expect a generic snooze-fest.

Not Testing and Iterating:

A single prompt may not get it perfect on the first go. Adjust, rephrase, and try again.

It's all a dance. And yes, sometimes you step on the AI's toes, but that's part of the fun.

Bonus Trick: Prompt Templates

Advanced users often create prompt templates — reusable structures that you can tweak for different tasks. It's like having a "mad libs" sheet for AI! For example:

"Act as a [profession]. Given the task '[task]', provide a detailed [type of output]. Keep the tone [tone]."

You just plug in the blanks depending on what you want. Super handy, especially when you're generating lots of content or need consistency.

Wrapping Up

Look, prompt engineering is a little bit of art, a little bit of science, and a whole lot of "talking nicely to robots." It's a skill that you develop the more you experiment and play. Sometimes you'll craft the perfect prompt and the AI will blow your mind. Other times you'll get something that makes you seriously question reality. Either way, you're learning.

And hey, the next time someone says "prompt engineering isn't real engineering," feel free to tell them you work in Linguistic Wizardry for Future Overlords. Sounds way cooler anyway.

Now grab your metaphorical toolbox, get creative, and start bossing those AIs around — politely, of course.

7.3 Summarization and Translation with AI

You ever wish you had a magical creature that could read an entire 400-page report and then tell you, in plain English, "Yeah, basically it says your company needs more coffee and fewer meetings"? Well, my friend, AI summarization is your new best buddy. And if that magical creature could also whisper translations in any language you want? That's the power combo we're diving into today — summarization and translation with generative AI. It's like having an intern who never sleeps, never complains, and somehow speaks fluent Japanese, Spanish, and Klingon (well, almost).

The truth is, machines have gotten freakishly good at both condensing huge amounts of information and hopping between languages. And unlike your old high school group project partner, they don't bail halfway through the task. They stay, they summarize, they translate — all with a smile. (Metaphorically. AI doesn't have faces. Yet.)

What is AI Summarization?

Alright, time to get a little more serious — but only slightly, I promise.

AI summarization is the process where a model reads a chunk of text (an article, a research paper, a 40-email-long email thread) and produces a shorter version that still captures the most important ideas. In tech-speak, there are two major types:

Extractive Summarization:

The AI selects key sentences or phrases from the original text and strings them together. It's like clipping highlights from a movie.

Abstractive Summarization:

The AI generates new sentences to express the main ideas, often paraphrasing or reorganizing information in its own words. It's more like retelling the story with flair.

Today's language models (like GPT, T5, and their friends) mostly do abstractive summarization — which makes the summaries sound more natural and less like Frankenstein's monster stitched from random sentences.

When and Why to Use Summarization

Summarization is insanely useful. Here's where it shines:

Research: Quickly understand dozens of scientific papers without losing your mind.

News: Get digestible snippets instead of scrolling through endless articles.

Business Reports: Executive summaries that make you look way smarter at meetings.

Customer Support: Summarize long complaint tickets into actionable points.

Basically, if it's too long and you didn't read it (TL;DR) — AI's got you.

And let's be real: In 2025 and beyond, time is the most valuable resource. Summarization gives you more of it.

What is AI Translation?

Now onto translation — the ancient art of getting "Where's the bathroom?" wrong in every country. Luckily, AI is making huge strides here too.

AI translation takes text written in one language and converts it into another while keeping the meaning intact. Unlike old-school word-for-word translations (that could turn "I'm full" into "I am pregnant" in some languages — yes, that happens), modern AI translation models focus on context and natural phrasing.

Systems like Google Translate, DeepL, and various LLMs now offer translations that are:

More fluent

More culturally appropriate

Less robotic-sounding

In fact, AI translators are now so good that in many professional settings, humans are just editing AI translations instead of starting from scratch.

Use Cases for AI Translation

Here's why AI translation is blowing up:

Global Business: Instantly localize marketing content, emails, and websites.

Education: Translate research papers, textbooks, and study materials.

Travel: Make reservations, navigate cities, and avoid accidentally ordering cow brains at restaurants.

Community Support: Help nonprofits or local governments communicate with multilingual communities.

Basically, if you're communicating with humans (and not just shouting into a void), translation matters.

How AI Models Handle Summarization and Translation

Here's the fun part: Modern AI can often handle both tasks with the same model — no need for separate apps.

For example, a large model like GPT-4 can:

Read a giant block of English text

Summarize it in two short paragraphs

Translate those paragraphs into Spanish, French, or even Swahili

All in one flow. Like a boss.

These models are trained on massive datasets containing tons of examples in different languages and writing styles. Through something called sequence-to-sequence learning, they learn how to predict outputs (like a summary or a translation) based on different types of inputs.

Bonus: Some newer models can summarize first, then translate, or translate first, then summarize — depending on what you need.

Quick Tips for Better AI Summarization and Translation

Want to look like a seasoned AI whisperer? Here are some pro tips:

For Summarization:

Specify the length ("Summarize in three sentences.")

Mention the style ("Make it sound professional" or "Explain like I'm five.")

Highlight key points you want to keep if necessary.

For Translation:

Tell the AI the tone you want ("formal business tone" vs "casual traveler's guide.")

Watch for idioms or slang — they can confuse even the smartest models.

Always do a quick sanity check on important translations (like legal contracts... seriously, don't just trust the robot on those).

Wrapping It All Up

Summarization and translation are two of the most practical, world-changing powers AI has given us. They save time, break down language barriers, and — let's be honest — make us look way more productive than we sometimes deserve.

And remember: AI is fast, tireless, and multilingual... but it's still not perfect. Think of it as your brilliant but slightly quirky sidekick, not a flawless wizard. Always keep a watchful human eye on the outputs — and maybe a good sense of humor, too.

Now, if you'll excuse me, I have a 60-page whitepaper to feed to my AI. In five minutes, I'll know if it's about blockchain, broccoli, or some horrifying new blockchain-powered broccoli startup. The future is wild. Let's ride.

7.4 Text Style Transfer and Creative Writing

Imagine if you could snap your fingers and instantly turn a boring corporate email into a Shakespearean sonnet. Or make your grocery list sound like it was written by Edgar Allan Poe. Well, my friend, welcome to the magical world of text style transfer — where AI takes a piece of writing and rewrites it in a totally different voice, tone, or style. It's basically a literary costume party, and trust me, things can get hilarious, weird, and ridiculously fun.

And if you're into creative writing — whether that's crafting short stories, scripting video game dialogues, or writing poems about sentient toasters — generative AI can be your brainstorming buddy, your co-author, or that weird friend who always has one too many plot twists. So buckle up, because we're about to get creative (and maybe a little weird, in the best way possible).

What is Text Style Transfer?

In formal, less goofy terms, text style transfer is when an AI model takes some text and rewrites it to match a new style without changing the original meaning too much.

For example:

Turning casual speech into formal writing

Changing modern English into old-timey Shakespearean English

Flipping positive reviews into sarcastic ones (or vice versa)

Gender-swapping or altering perspective (first-person to third-person)

Basically, it's like telling the AI: "Hey, say the same thing, but put on this different hat while you're at it."

This works because modern language models, like GPT-based systems, have been trained on mountains of text in a variety of styles, voices, and tones. They're like that friend who can do scary-accurate impressions of anyone after five minutes.

How Does AI Actually Pull This Off?

Without turning this into a computer science lecture (because nobody brought coffee), here's the short version:

Understanding Context:

First, the AI reads the original text and figures out what it's about — the "content."

Identifying Target Style:

Based on the prompt you give ("Make it sound like a pirate"), the model adjusts its word choices, sentence structure, tone, and even rhythm to fit.

Regenerating the Output:

The model then writes new sentences that carry the same meaning but sound different, based on the style you asked for.

Pretty slick, right?

Some more advanced models can even do multi-attribute transfers — like making text both more formal and more positive at the same time.

Why Does Text Style Transfer Matter?

Besides the obvious "it's super cool" reason, there are serious, practical uses for style transfer too:

Content Creation: Repackaging blog posts for different audiences (professional vs casual).

Marketing: Tailoring ads to different demographics or social media platforms.

Education: Helping students rewrite essays to improve tone or clarity.

Accessibility: Adjusting complex texts for easier reading levels.

Entertainment: Creating parodies, pastiches, or experimental art.

Also... it's really, really fun. Did I mention that? Because turning government policies into pirate speak is, frankly, an underappreciated life joy.

AI and Creative Writing: The Dream Team

If text style transfer is the costume party, creative writing with AI is the wild storytelling afterparty.

Generative models can:

Spin out story ideas

Help brainstorm plots

Build character profiles

Write dialogue in specific voices

Suggest plot twists you'd never think of (sometimes delightfully insane ones)

The beauty is that AI doesn't have writer's block. It doesn't get tired, or insecure, or stuck wondering if its metaphors are any good. (Although, side note, it will occasionally write the cheesiest love scenes imaginable. Be warned.)

The key to using AI for creative writing isn't just pushing the "generate" button and walking away. It's collaborating. Think of it as co-writing with a really enthusiastic alien who knows all the tropes but none of the clichés.

Tips for Using AI in Style Transfer and Creative Writing

Wanna look like a pro who totally has their creative act together? Here's a few friendly tips:

Be Specific with Prompts:

"Rewrite this in the style of a noir detective novel" will get you way better results than just "make it different."

Layer Instructions:

Combine tone, genre, and voice for more complex style shifts. (Example: "Summarize this email in a funny, sarcastic tone, like a tired sitcom character.")

Iterate:

Don't expect the first output to be perfect. Nudge, tweak, and re-prompt. It's a back-and-forth dance, not a one-click magic spell.

Blend AI Output with Human Flair:

Let AI throw out the first messy draft, then polish it with your own creativity. Best of both worlds.

Use It to Break Creative Blocks:

Stuck on a scene or a story idea? Ask the AI to give you five options for what happens next. You don't have to use them, but they might spark something brilliant.

Real-World Examples

Style Transfer:

A brand takes a stiff product description ("Our widget uses advanced nanotechnology to improve productivity.") and reworks it into a fun, casual tagline ("This widget's got nano-magic that saves you so much time you'll wonder if you invented a time machine.") — using AI.

Creative Writing:

A sci-fi writer uses an AI to generate different endings for a dystopian novel. Some endings are too weird (turns out everyone's a space duck?), but a few give the perfect "aha!" moment for the final scene.

Wrapping Up

Text style transfer and creative writing with AI aren't about replacing human writers — they're about turbocharging your imagination. The AI isn't here to steal your pen (or keyboard); it's here to be the nerdy, excitable brainstorm buddy you never knew you needed.

And hey, even if your AI-generated vampire romance novel where everyone's secretly a sentient donut doesn't win the Pulitzer... it'll definitely win my heart.

Now go forth, brave writer. Swap styles, break genres, make something so ridiculous and brilliant that even your toaster would be impressed.

7.5 Ethical Considerations in Text Generation

Alright, grab your moral compass, your thinking cap, and maybe a snack, because this part of the AI journey gets deep. Up until now, we've been having a blast making AI write poems, stories, summaries, and Shakespearean grocery lists. But here's the deal: with great power (and hilarious AI-generated limericks) comes great responsibility. Welcome to Ethical Considerations in Text Generation — where we talk about the "should we" instead of just the "can we."

And don't worry, I'll try not to make it sound like a boring legal lecture. We'll keep it real, and maybe even a little fun, because ethics doesn't have to feel like watching paint dry.

Why Ethics Even Matters in Text Generation

Let's set the stage: Imagine you build an amazing AI that can write convincing news articles in seconds. Sounds awesome, right?

Now imagine someone uses it to create fake news about, say, a celebrity adopting a pet alien. Or worse — spreading harmful lies about real people or events.

That's why ethics matters.

When AI models generate text, they have the power to inform, influence, or mislead millions — often faster than any human could. It's like handing out megaphones to everyone... including people who maybe, just maybe, shouldn't have a megaphone.

So whether you're training models, using them, or just cheering from the sidelines, it's crucial to think about how the tools are used and what they might cause.

Key Ethical Issues in Text Generation

Let's dive into some of the hot-button issues without sounding like a philosophy textbook:

1. Misinformation and Disinformation

AI models can whip up realistic-sounding news stories, tweets, blog posts — you name it.

The danger? They can just as easily generate false or misleading content. Sometimes unintentionally (hallucination errors), and sometimes because people ask them to.

In the wrong hands, AI could flood the internet with garbage faster than a toddler let loose in a glitter factory.

Solution: Always fact-check AI outputs, especially when the content relates to news, health, finance, or politics.

2. Bias and Fairness

Here's a not-so-fun fact: AI models often inherit the biases of the data they were trained on.

If a model has seen more positive news stories about certain groups and more negative stories about others, it can unintentionally reflect those biases in its writing.

Example? Gender stereotypes, racial bias, cultural misrepresentations — yeah, they can all sneak in if you're not careful.

Solution: Use diverse, balanced training datasets. Audit outputs regularly. Be mindful of unintended slants or stereotypes.

3. Copyright and Ownership

If an AI model "learns" from millions of copyrighted books, articles, and tweets, who owns what it creates?

Is the new text truly original? Or is it remixing and regurgitating someone else's protected work?

Spoiler: the legal world is still figuring this out. But as creators and users, we need to think about whether we're respecting original authors or just, you know, stealing politely.

Solution: Understand copyright laws in your region. When using AI-generated content commercially, be cautious and consider adding human revisions.

4. Privacy Concerns

Ever hear about AI models accidentally spitting out real people's personal data? Yeah, it happens.

If a model trains on exposed datasets (say, leaked emails or public forums), it might "remember" and regurgitate private information.

Solution: Train models responsibly on properly scrubbed datasets. Always prioritize data privacy and user confidentiality.

5. Over-Reliance and Human Displacement

Look, I love AI. I've basically spent 20 years hanging out with it.

But we shouldn't pretend that it can (or should) replace all human creativity and jobs.

If businesses think, "Why hire a writer when I can get free blog posts from a robot?" — we risk devaluing human craftsmanship, subtlety, and, you know... soul.

Solution: Use AI to augment human skills, not replace them. Humans bring empathy, ethics, and creativity that AI just can't fake. (Yet. And if it ever can, we'll have bigger problems.)

Setting Some Ground Rules: Ethical Best Practices

Here's my quick and dirty checklist for keeping things ethically awesome when working with AI-generated text:

Transparency:

Let people know when they're reading AI-generated content.

Accountability:

Take responsibility for the outputs you share. "The AI made me do it" isn't a good excuse.

Moderation:

Especially on platforms with user-generated content, have systems in place to catch harmful AI output.

Human in the Loop:

Always have a real person reviewing important AI outputs — especially for sensitive topics.

Continuous Learning:

Ethics isn't a one-time box to check. Stay updated as laws, guidelines, and social norms evolve.

Real-World Examples (Because Stories Make Everything Better)

The Good:

AI models used to help researchers quickly summarize COVID-19 papers during the pandemic, speeding up life-saving discoveries.

The Bad:

Deepfake articles pretending to be written by journalists who didn't exist, spreading political propaganda.

The Ugly:

A chatbot accidentally encouraging self-harm because no one trained it on crisis response scenarios.

Wrapping It Up

Look, at the end of the day, AI is like a hyper-energetic puppy. It can fetch your slippers, it can destroy your favorite couch, and it's entirely up to you to train it right.

Text generation is an amazing, powerful tool — a revolution for creativity, learning, business, and beyond. But if we don't guide it carefully, it can just as easily cause harm as it can inspire.

So let's build a future where AI-generated words uplift, connect, and empower people — not confuse, mislead, or hurt them.

And if in doubt? Remember the ancient wisdom of the internet: Don't be a jerk.

Now, who's ready to use AI responsibly and still have a blast doing it? (Raises hand enthusiastically.)

Chapter 8: Generative AI for Images

Now we enter the world where pixels become paintings and noise becomes nature scenes. This is the playground for AI artists—and you're about to become one. Whether it's designing surreal landscapes or turning selfies into anime portraits, this chapter unleashes your inner Da Vinci (or DALL·E).

In this chapter, you'll learn the basics of image generation and synthesis. We'll explore how GANs create realistic visuals, experiment with style transfer, and discuss tools like DeepDream and Stable Diffusion. Techniques for fine-tuning image output and ensuring visual quality are also included, along with creative and commercial use cases.

8.1 Image Generation Basics

Alright, if you thought getting a computer to write poetry was magical, wait till you see it paint. Welcome to the dazzling world of Image Generation Basics, where your computer learns to whip up images out of thin air — no paintbrush, no messy palettes, and definitely no beret required (though wearing one for dramatic flair is highly encouraged).
We're about to dive into how machines take nothing but math and data, and somehow poof — realistic cats, futuristic cities, or even totally new art styles appear. It's like teaching your toaster to sculpt Michelangelo's David... only cooler and slightly less crumbly.

What Does Image Generation Mean?

In simple terms, image generation means training a computer to create pictures — from scratch or by transforming existing images. These pictures can be photorealistic (like a face that doesn't exist but looks frighteningly real) or wildly artistic (like a unicorn riding a bicycle across Saturn's rings).

The key difference between "normal" image editing and "generative" image creation is that generative models actually invent new content, not just modify what's already there.

Imagine telling a machine:

"Hey, dream up a new type of bird that looks like it belongs on Mars."

And instead of Googling it, the AI actually invents that bird for you. Mind-blowing, right?

How Does a Computer Learn to Generate Images?

Short version:

It gets fed a LOT of images first. Thousands, sometimes millions.

Think of it like showing a toddler millions of photos of animals and then asking them to draw a "new" animal.

Here's the rough play-by-play:

Training:

The AI looks at mountains of existing images and learns their features — colors, shapes, patterns, textures, lighting, proportions, etc.

Understanding Patterns:

It doesn't memorize individual pictures; instead, it learns underlying structures. Like: "cats usually have two triangle ears and are fuzzy" or "mountains tend to have jagged tops."

Generating New Images:

Once trained, it can remix all those patterns into completely new images that fit the learned "rules" but aren't just copies.

It's a little like how musicians listen to tons of music, learn the "rules" of melody and rhythm, and then start making their own songs.

Core Techniques Behind Image Generation

Okay, let's name-drop a few superstar techniques without making your eyes glaze over:

Generative Adversarial Networks (GANs):

Two neural networks compete — one tries to create realistic images, and the other tries to catch the faker. They push each other until the generated images become eerily convincing.

(It's basically AI bootcamp.)

Variational Autoencoders (VAEs):

These models learn to compress images into a "code" and then decompress them — and during that process, they can create entirely new variations.

Diffusion Models:

A newer trend where AI starts with random noise and gradually "sculpts" it into an image, kind of like carving a statue out of a block of marble (but fuzzier and with more math).

Each method has strengths and tradeoffs — GANs are fantastic at realism, VAEs at smooth generation, and diffusion models at producing incredibly detailed, coherent images.

The Role of Datasets

Behind every impressive AI artwork, there's a dataset quietly doing the heavy lifting. Datasets for image generation are huge, diverse, and cover everything from cats to castles to cartoon clowns.

Popular datasets include:

ImageNet: Millions of labeled images across thousands of categories.

COCO (Common Objects in Context): Real-world images, labeled with the objects inside them.

LAION-5B: A massive dataset of images paired with text captions (perfect for models like Stable Diffusion).

These datasets teach the model what things are and how they typically look, helping the AI build a mental "library" of the world.

Challenges in Image Generation

Before you start thinking AI is perfect at this, let's be real: it still struggles sometimes.

Weird anatomy:

Hands with six fingers. People with two noses. Dogs with... way too many legs.

AI can sometimes mash concepts together in hilariously wrong ways.

Bias and Stereotypes:

If the training data is skewed (say, only showing certain types of people or places), the AI's outputs can be biased too.

Compute Hunger:

Training powerful image generators can require ridiculous amounts of computing power — like "could toast a loaf of bread with the heat from the servers" levels of power.

Overfitting:

Sometimes, models memorize too much instead of learning the patterns, leading to images that look too similar to training examples.

But the field is advancing fast — and newer models are getting crazier good at dodging these pitfalls.

Real-World Applications

Image generation isn't just for making memes (although, yes, it's amazing for that too).

Here's where it's making real waves:

Entertainment:

Creating concept art for movies, video games, and comics.

Marketing and Branding:

Generating custom ad visuals without the need for expensive photoshoots.

Fashion Design:

Dreaming up entirely new clothing styles and textures.

Medical Imaging:

Enhancing scans, creating training data for rare conditions.

Scientific Visualization:

Helping researchers visualize molecules, planets, or complex systems.

And honestly? We're just scratching the surface.

Final Thoughts

Learning how to generate images with AI is like getting your own army of slightly drunk but very enthusiastic artists. Sometimes they'll paint a masterpiece, and sometimes they'll give you a horse with three heads.

Either way — it's ridiculously fun, endlessly fascinating, and the future of creative work is already here.

So next time you see an AI-generated picture and think, "Wow, that's amazing!" — remember: behind that masterpiece was a ton of training, a lot of probability calculations... and maybe a few AI faceplants along the way.

Now buckle up, because next, we're going even deeper into how these magic tricks work under the hood.
(And don't worry, I packed extra humor for the journey.)

8.2 Intro to GANs for Image Synthesis

When I first heard about GANs (Generative Adversarial Networks), I thought it sounded like some underground hacker gang that meets at midnight in shady cafés. Turns out, it's even cooler: it's a type of AI that basically teaches itself to become an incredible artist — by lying to itself. Seriously, if machines could grow up, GANs would be the rebellious teenagers of AI.

Today, we're going to break down what GANs are, why they're absolutely mind-blowing for image synthesis, and why even after 20 years in this field, they still make me geek out like a kid at a candy store.

What Are GANs, Really?

Imagine two AIs locked in an endless battle:

One (the Generator) tries to create fake images — realistic enough to fool someone.

The other (the Discriminator) acts like a tough art critic, trying to spot every fake the Generator throws at it.

Every time the Generator messes up (like drawing a dog with six ears), the Discriminator catches it.

Every time the Generator gets closer to making a realistic image, the Discriminator gets sharper, harder to fool.

And around and around they go, improving each other until the Generator becomes so good that even the Discriminator can barely tell what's real.

In short: GANs are a game of high-stakes forgery and detection, and through this adversarial process, machines learn to produce stunningly realistic images.

Birth of GANs

GANs were first introduced by Ian Goodfellow in 2014, and let me tell you — the field of AI basically had a mic drop moment right then.

Up until then, machine-generated images mostly looked like pixelated nightmares. After GANs? Suddenly, AI could create human faces that didn't even exist — and you wouldn't know the difference.

It was one of those "before and after" moments for AI — like going from doodling stick figures to painting a Rembrandt overnight.

How the GAN Architecture Works

Let's break it down without frying our brains, shall we?

Generator:

Takes in random noise (like static on a TV screen) and tries to convert it into a meaningful image — say, a cat or a car.

Discriminator:

Looks at images and tries to guess: "Is this real (from the dataset) or fake (made by the Generator)?"

Both networks train together.

If the Discriminator catches a fake, it sends feedback.

If the Generator tricks the Discriminator, it celebrates (and secretly levels up its skills).

Over time, they both get ridiculously good at their jobs.

This dynamic is what makes GANs so powerful — it's not just one model getting better, it's two models pushing each other to new heights.

Why Are GANs So Good for Image Synthesis?

Three big reasons:

Detail and Sharpness:

GANs excel at creating incredibly detailed images. Whether it's the texture of skin, the glint of light in an eye, or the fuzziness of a kitten's fur, GANs capture tiny nuances.

High Realism:

Properly trained GANs can generate images so realistic they're virtually indistinguishable from real photos — no Photoshop needed.

Flexibility:

You can guide GANs to generate specific types of images: anime characters, street scenes, fashion models, even imaginary landscapes from alien worlds.

It's like giving an AI the brush and saying, "Surprise me," and somehow getting the Mona Lisa riding a skateboard.

Different Flavors of GANs

GANs aren't just one-size-fits-all. Over the years, researchers have developed lots of GAN variants, each with their own twists:

DCGAN (Deep Convolutional GAN):

Uses convolutional layers, perfect for generating high-quality, detailed images.

Conditional GAN (cGAN):

Allows you to "condition" the generation — for instance, generate only images of cats if you tell it "cat."

CycleGAN:

Specializes in translating one type of image to another — like turning horses into zebras or summer scenes into winter wonderlands.

StyleGAN (and StyleGAN2, StyleGAN3):

Some of the most advanced models yet — capable of producing ultra-realistic human faces and even letting you tweak individual features (e.g., adding a smile or changing the hair color).

Each of these has special talents, and depending on what you need, you pick the right "flavor" of GAN.

Challenges with GANs

Oh, you thought it was all sunshine and perfectly rendered puppies?
GANs have their own drama too:

Training Instability:

GANs can collapse if not trained carefully, leading to terrible results (think images that look like cursed relics from a horror movie).

Mode Collapse:

Sometimes the Generator gets lazy and keeps producing only one or a few types of images.

Need for Massive Data:

GANs typically need huge datasets and a lot of training time to reach their true potential.

Sensitivity to Hyperparameters:

Tiny tweaks (like learning rate changes) can make or break a GAN's training process.

Think of GAN training like taming a wild horse: it can take off in weird directions if you're not careful.

Real-World Magic with GANs

Here's how GANs are making waves outside of research labs:

Fashion:

Brands generate new clothing designs based on trends without ever sewing a stitch.

Art:

AI artists are using GANs to create completely original pieces that sell for real money (sometimes six figures).

Gaming:

Creating massive amounts of realistic textures, faces, and environments procedurally.

Medical Imaging:

Augmenting datasets by creating synthetic images, which helps in training better diagnostic models without privacy concerns.

GANs have gone from academic curiosity to the Swiss Army Knife of the creative AI world.

Final Thoughts

If Machine Learning is the party, then GANs are that wild, chaotic genius who shows up fashionably late, makes a mess, but ends up being the life of the whole event.

They're unpredictable, challenging to work with, but when they succeed — holy smokes, they produce jaw-dropping results.

So next time you see a ridiculously realistic photo and wonder if it's real or AI-made, just remember: somewhere behind the curtain, a Generator and a Discriminator were locked in an epic battle of creative one-upmanship... and you, my friend, get to enjoy the masterpiece they fought to create.

Now, hold onto your hat, because in the next chapter, we'll tackle Style Transfer — where art meets AI in the most mind-bending ways possible!

8.3 Style Transfer Techniques

When I first saw style transfer in action, I thought the AI had become a wizard overnight. One minute it's a plain photo of a boring street corner, and the next — BAM! — it's dripping in the neon chaos of a Van Gogh fever dream. Honestly, if AI ever got a side hustle, it would probably open an art gallery and charge us admission.

Today, my friends, we're diving into the magical, colorful world of style transfer — where your selfie gets a Picasso makeover, and your dog photo ends up looking like a scene from "Starry Night."

What Is Style Transfer?

At its heart, style transfer is about taking two images — one as the content (the thing you're painting) and one as the style (the way you paint it) — and blending them together into a single masterpiece.

Imagine snapping a photo of your morning coffee and making it look like it was painted by Monet — shimmering reflections and all. That's style transfer:

It keeps the shapes and structure of your original image.

It adopts the texture, color, and brushstrokes of the artistic style image.

In technical terms, it's all about matching the content representation of one image with the style representation of another — but we'll save the heavy math for another day. You and I? We're here to make magic.

How Does Style Transfer Actually Work?

Alright, let's nerd out for just a second.

Style transfer typically uses Convolutional Neural Networks (CNNs) — the same types of networks that are great at recognizing cats, dogs, and suspiciously photogenic avocados.

Here's the (simplified) recipe:

Content Extraction:

A pre-trained CNN (like VGG-19) looks at your original photo and figures out the important stuff — edges, shapes, layout. This becomes your "content map."

Style Extraction:

The same CNN analyzes a famous artwork (say, a Picasso painting) and identifies patterns in texture, color usage, and brushstroke styles. This becomes your "style map."

Optimization:

Now, using a random noise image as a starting point, the model tweaks and tunes the pixels until it captures both:

The structure of your original photo

The look and feel of the style image

The optimization process juggles two loss functions: one for content and one for style. It's a bit like trying to sculpt a statue with both your eyes closed and someone tickling you — tricky but possible.

Types of Style Transfer

You didn't think there was just one flavor, did you? Oh no. Style transfer techniques come in different styles (pun 100% intended):

Original Neural Style Transfer (Gatys et al.):

The classic, slow but high-quality version. You optimize a new image from scratch using backpropagation.

Fast Style Transfer:

Train a network to learn a specific style so that it can apply it to any image instantly. Way faster, though usually a tiny bit less accurate.

Arbitrary Style Transfer:

Newer methods can apply any style to any content without retraining. Examples include AdaIN (Adaptive Instance Normalization) and StyleSwap.

Photorealistic Style Transfer:

Focuses on preserving realism while applying subtle stylistic changes. Great for keeping things looking believable instead of like a fever dream.

Each method has its pros and cons, but they all share the same goal: make ordinary images extraordinary.

Popular Applications of Style Transfer

If you're wondering where this tech shows up outside of "cool Instagram filters," buckle up:

Social Media Filters:

Ever turned yourself into a painting with just one tap? Thank style transfer.

Movie Industry:

Directors are using AI-driven style transfer to create unique, stylized looks for entire scenes without months of manual editing.

Gaming:

Developers apply specific art styles across whole game worlds, saving thousands of artist hours.

Personalized Art Gifts:

People upload their photos, pick a style (like "paint me in the style of Da Vinci"), and get custom posters, mugs, or T-shirts.

Augmented Reality (AR):

Live video filters use style transfer to change how reality looks — in real-time.

Basically, if it's cool, artsy, and somewhere on the internet — style transfer probably had a hand in it.

Challenges in Style Transfer

Of course, no great power comes without a few headaches:

Maintaining Content:

Too much stylization and suddenly your adorable puppy looks like an abstract blob.

Generalization:

Many models struggle when applying styles to images they weren't trained on.

Real-Time Constraints:

Achieving good-looking style transfer in live video requires serious optimization.

Preserving Colors:

Sometimes style transfer warps the colors of your original photo too much, making things look...well, weird.

But hey, a little weirdness is a small price to pay for turning your grocery store parking lot into a Renaissance masterpiece.

How to Try Style Transfer Yourself

Good news: you don't need a PhD or a supercomputer!

Some easy ways to dip your toes in:

Google Colab Notebooks:

Tons of free style transfer notebooks online let you upload two images and watch the magic happen.

Mobile Apps:

Apps like Prisma, DeepArt, and Painnt let you do style transfer with just a few taps.

Python Libraries:

If you're feeling brave, libraries like TensorFlow and PyTorch have pre-built models you can play with — and tweak if you're feeling fancy.

A few lines of code (or a few taps on your phone), and you'll have your dog looking like he just stepped out of a Dali painting.

Final Thoughts

Style transfer is one of those fields that reminds me why I fell in love with AI in the first place: it's creative, surprising, and just a little bit rebellious.

It doesn't want to just recognize patterns — it wants to remix, repaint, and reimagine the world around it.

And if that's not peak AI energy, I don't know what is.

So go ahead: grab your favorite selfie, mash it together with your favorite painting, and unleash your inner artist. Worst case scenario? You accidentally create the next art movement and confuse a whole generation.

Best case? You confuse two generations.

Next up, we're going even deeper — exploring Deep Dream and those wild, trippy filters that make even your cat look like it's seeing into another dimension. Get ready, because it's about to get psychedelic.

8.4 Deep Dream and Artistic Filters

When I first heard about Deep Dream, I honestly thought it was a sci-fi movie where computers finally started dreaming of electric sheep (thanks, Philip K. Dick). Turns out, I wasn't too far off.

Deep Dream is what happens when you ask a neural network, "Hey buddy, what do you see here?" and it responds by hallucinating a kaleidoscope of dog faces, weird eyes, and swirling patterns all over your photo. Spoiler alert: it's both mesmerizing and mildly terrifying.

Today, let's dive into the weird, wonderful world of Deep Dream and artistic filters — where reality takes a vacation and your AI buddy takes a very strange creative turn.

What Is Deep Dream?

Deep Dream is like neural networks on a psychedelic road trip.

Originally created by engineers at Google in 2015, Deep Dream started as a way to visualize what neural networks were learning inside their many mysterious layers.

Here's the basic idea:

You feed an image into a trained convolutional neural network (CNN).

Instead of using it to classify the image (like "this is a cat"), you encourage the network to amplify the patterns it recognizes.

It picks up on textures, shapes, and colors, then enhances them over and over — creating wild, surreal images filled with exaggerated features.

At its core, Deep Dream isn't about creating new things from scratch — it's about taking tiny signals from an image and turning them up to 11 until everything looks like it's melting and growing dog snouts.

How Does Deep Dream Work?

Let's walk through it without melting your brain:

Pre-Trained Network:

You start with a neural network already trained on millions of images (like InceptionV3).

Layer Selection:

You pick a layer (or several) from the network. Early layers see simple shapes like edges; deeper layers see complex stuff like dog faces or buildings.

Gradient Ascent:

Normally in training, we minimize loss. In Deep Dream, we do the opposite — we maximize the activation of certain features by tweaking the input image itself.

Feedback Loop:

As you tweak the image, those features grow stronger and more defined. The more iterations you do, the weirder (and sometimes cooler) the results get.

In simple terms: the network "dreams" harder and harder about what it thinks it sees in your image — and it can get wild fast.

Deep Dream vs Regular Artistic Filters

You might be thinking, "Isn't this just another Instagram filter?" Oh no, my friend. It's weirder than that.

Artistic filters (like Prisma or Photoshop effects) are usually pre-designed transformations. You pick a filter and it applies a known set of changes.

Deep Dream, on the other hand, is dynamic. It changes based on the input image, the chosen network layer, and even random factors. No two Deep Dreams are the same.

In short: filters give you a look.

Deep Dream gives you a hallucination.

Popular Artistic Filters and Tools

While Deep Dream is its own beast, the boom in AI art opened the door to many other artistic filters and enhancements:

Neural Style Transfer Filters:

Apps like Prisma, DeepArt, and Painnt made it super easy to blend famous art styles into your photos.

Real-Time Artistic Filters:

Snap Camera, Instagram, and TikTok use lightweight AI models to give you face-swap filters, cartoon looks, and surreal backgrounds on the fly.

AI-Powered Photo Enhancers:

Tools like Remini and Let's Enhance use AI to upscale, sharpen, and even reimagine your blurry photos.

If Deep Dream is the weird artist painting in the corner at 3 a.m., these other tools are the polished professionals giving your images a glow-up.

How You Can Play with Deep Dream

The best part? You don't have to work at Google to mess with Deep Dream anymore. Here's how to get your psychedelic artist on:

Google's Deep Dream Generator:

A free online tool where you upload your photo, pick a style, and let the magic happen.

DeepDream Python Libraries:

If you're feeling fancy (and know a bit of Python), libraries like TensorFlow and PyTorch have tutorials for building your own Deep Dream generator from scratch.

Mobile Apps:

Several mobile apps let you Deep Dreamify your photos without writing a single line of code.

Pro tip: start subtle. A little dreaming can make your photo beautifully surreal. Too much dreaming and your grandma's portrait will have fifteen extra eyeballs.

Creative Uses of Deep Dream and Artistic Filters

Sure, it's fun to turn your cat into a cosmic spaghetti monster — but Deep Dream and artistic filters have legit creative uses too:

Album Covers:

Musicians have used Deep Dream art for album covers and promotional posters.

Fashion:

Designers are exploring AI-generated patterns for clothes and textiles.

Movies and Visual Effects:

Some indie films use style transfer and Deep Dream to create trippy dream sequences.

Therapeutic Art:

Art therapists sometimes use AI-transformed imagery to help clients explore abstract emotions and thoughts.

Basically, it's not just for memes (although, let's be honest, memes are a pretty good use).

Challenges and Limitations

Of course, no AI magic trick comes without its fine print:

Loss of Original Content:

Deep Dream can warp your image so much that it's unrecognizable.

Compute Heavy:

Generating high-quality Deep Dream art can be resource-intensive.

Over-Saturation:

The novelty can wear off quickly if every photo starts looking like a Dali painting at a rave.

Interpretability:

Sometimes it's just... too weird. Like, "is that a banana or a goat wearing sunglasses?" weird.

But hey, a little weirdness is good for the soul.

Final Thoughts

Deep Dream and artistic filters remind me that AI isn't just about automation and optimization — it's about imagination.

When we let machines dream, we tap into something beautifully unpredictable and deeply human: the urge to create, remix, and reimagine the world around us.

And if that means occasionally seeing a dog-faced tree in your vacation photos, well... that's a price I'm willing to pay.

Next up, we'll get even fancier — diving into Stable Diffusion, where AI generation gets a whole lot more realistic and way less psychedelic (well... usually). Stay tuned, and keep dreaming!

8.5 Stable Diffusion for Realistic Image Output

When I first heard the phrase "Stable Diffusion," I thought it was a shampoo for horses. Seriously. Turns out, it's not about haircare for majestic creatures — it's about one of the coolest, mind-blowingly powerful technologies in the world of AI image generation today.

If Deep Dream is like an AI on a psychedelic trip, Stable Diffusion is like a super-talented digital artist who just had four cups of coffee and can paint anything you describe — from "a cat riding a skateboard on Mars" to "a photorealistic portrait of a cyberpunk knight sipping bubble tea."

Let's saddle up (pun intended) and dive deep into how Stable Diffusion is changing the way we think about creating realistic images with AI.

What is Stable Diffusion?

Stable Diffusion is an open-source, latent diffusion model developed by Stability AI, CompVis, and others.

In plain English: it's an AI model that can generate high-quality images from text prompts (or even modify existing images) in an efficient and... well, stable way.

What makes it special?

Text-to-Image: You give it a description, it gives you an image. It's like ordering art from a cosmic takeout menu.

High Quality: It can create stunning, detailed, realistic images that often look better than some professional stock photos.

Open-Source: Unlike models locked behind giant tech walls, Stable Diffusion is open for everyone — artists, researchers, hobbyists, and chaos goblins alike.

Efficient: It can run on personal hardware (if you've got a decent GPU) instead of needing an entire data center.

In short, it democratized the power of AI image generation, handing it to the masses. And boy, did the masses run with it.

How Stable Diffusion Works (Without Melting Your Brain)

Okay, so how does it actually do the magic? Here's the non-scary version:

Latent Space:

- Instead of working directly on full-size images, Stable Diffusion compresses them into a smaller, hidden representation (called "latent space").
- Think of it like sketching a rough outline before doing a full oil painting.

Diffusion Process:

- The model starts with pure noise — basically static — and gradually denoises it step-by-step, guided by your text prompt.
- Imagine taking a fuzzy TV screen and slowly turning it into a beautiful landscape painting.

Guidance:

- Your text prompt "guides" the model about what features to pull out from the noise.
- Say "an astronaut reading a book in a jungle," and the model literally brings that to life, combining the elements in surreal but logical ways.

It's like reverse chaos — starting from total randomness and sculpting it into something stunning.

Why Stable Diffusion is a Game-Changer

- Before Stable Diffusion, access to high-quality text-to-image models was limited to big players like OpenAI (with DALL·E) or closed beta programs.
- Stable Diffusion flipped the table and shouted, "Hey! Let's make this art party public!"

Creative Freedom:

Artists could create wild fantasy scenes, photorealistic portraits, or trippy album covers with just a few lines of text.

Customization:

Thanks to its open-source nature, people trained custom models on their own styles, characters, or concepts.

Innovation Explosion:

New apps, tools, and workflows popped up overnight — AI image editors, upscalers, dream journals, storytelling apps, even video generators.

It wasn't just a tech shift. It was a cultural earthquake.

Some Fun Things You Can Do with Stable Diffusion

Let's be honest, part of the joy is just seeing what absurd prompts you can throw at it. But beyond the memes, here's what Stable Diffusion can do:

Create Artwork from Prompts:

Describe your wildest ideas and get visual masterpieces.

Image-to-Image Translation:

Upload a sketch or photo, add a prompt, and transform it into a new version (more realistic, more cartoonish, more cyberpunk).

Inpainting:

Edit parts of an image by telling the AI what you want in a specific area — perfect for fixing, enhancing, or creatively altering images.

Style Transfer:

Apply artistic styles — Van Gogh, anime, sci-fi — to your images.

Character and Concept Art:

Build consistent, themed characters for books, games, or comics.

It's like having a magic art studio in your laptop.

Important Tips for Using Stable Diffusion

If you're itching to start generating your own masterpieces, a few pro tips from the trenches:

Prompt Engineering Matters:

Better prompts = better images. Be specific. Add details like style ("in the style of Studio Ghibli") or mood ("dark, eerie, misty forest").

Learn Negative Prompts:

You can tell the AI what you don't want (like "no blurry faces" or "no text") for cleaner results.

Adjust Settings:

Tweak things like guidance scale (how strictly it follows your prompt) and inference steps (how many times it refines the image).

Hardware Considerations:

A decent GPU speeds things up. Without one, online services and platforms like DreamStudio, Hugging Face Spaces, or local installs with "low VRAM mode" can help.

Challenges and Ethical Considerations

As always with great power comes... weirdness.

Bias and Stereotypes:

AI models sometimes reflect biases from the data they were trained on.

Copyright Issues:

If the model learned from copyrighted works, there's a gray area about using or selling AI-generated content.

Misuse:

Fake imagery, deepfakes, and misleading content are real concerns.

Creators and developers are still figuring out how to balance open innovation with responsible use — and it's a conversation we all need to be part of.

Final Thoughts

Stable Diffusion is like giving your imagination a flamethrower. You can light up entire new worlds — or accidentally set your backyard on fire. (Please don't actually set your backyard on fire.)

It's powerful, fun, sometimes overwhelming, but ultimately an incredible creative tool that's only just getting started.

Whether you're an artist, a writer, a marketer, or just someone who likes seeing "a disco robot riding a unicorn" brought to life, Stable Diffusion puts magic at your fingertips.

Now, if you'll excuse me, I have to go generate an image of "an avocado wizard battling a pizza dragon under a rainbow." You know, for science.

Chapter 9: Real-World Applications of Generative AI

Remember when AI was just a sci-fi subplot? Well, now it's designing fashion, composing music, writing ad copy, and maybe even ghostwriting your favorite influencer's tweets. This chapter zooms out and shows how generative AI is crashing into reality—and bringing snacks.

We'll examine major industry use cases across entertainment, education, marketing, healthcare, and interactive technologies like chatbots and AR/VR. This chapter offers a broad perspective on how businesses and creators are leveraging generative AI to innovate and optimize, as well as the opportunities and challenges that come with mainstream adoption.

9.1 AI in Entertainment and Media

You know, when I first thought about AI in entertainment, I pictured a robot telling jokes in a smoky stand-up comedy club. (Spoiler: the robot was surprisingly bad at knock-knock jokes but crushed it with existential humor.)

Fast forward to today, and AI isn't just cracking awkward jokes — it's rewriting scripts, composing music, designing video games, creating visual effects, and even "acting" in movies. Seriously, it's like Hollywood opened the floodgates and said, "Come on in, bots, the water's warm!"

Now let's break down exactly how AI is jazz-handing its way into entertainment and media — and why it's not slowing down anytime soon.

The Rise of AI Storytelling

AI is no longer just a tool — it's becoming a co-creator.

Scriptwriting and Screenplays:

AI models like OpenAI's GPT-family are helping writers brainstorm, generate dialogue, and even plot entire screenplays. Imagine tossing a prompt like "A detective in space falls in love with a ghost" into an AI, and getting a rough story outline within minutes. It's not always perfect, but it's a goldmine for breaking writer's block.

Video Game Narrative Engines:

Games are now using AI to generate branching dialogue trees and dynamic storylines. Instead of manually scripting every possible interaction, AI helps create massive, immersive worlds with responsive characters.
Games like AI Dungeon proved that players want worlds where anything they imagine can happen — and AI makes that scale possible.

AI and Music: Beats by Bots

Remember when the idea of a robot writing music sounded like a dystopian joke? Yeah... now AI can:

Compose original scores.

Generate beats for pop, rap, or electronic music.

Remix songs into entirely new styles.

Even master tracks for professional quality.

Tools like Amper Music, AIVA, and Soundraw let creators whip up background scores for films, ads, or YouTube videos without needing a full orchestra or a second mortgage.

Fun fact: AI-generated music has already been nominated for awards. So yeah, your future Grammy competition might just be an algorithm named Kevin.

Visual Effects, Animation, and AI Magic

Visual effects (VFX) and animation studios are embracing AI faster than a cat chasing a laser pointer.

Deepfake Technology:

Used responsibly, deepfakes can de-age actors, resurrect historical figures, or create stunning character transformations without months of manual labor. (Used irresponsibly... well, that's a whole other conversation.)

Image Upscaling:

AI models like ESRGAN upscale low-resolution images and videos to HD or 4K without losing quality. This means remastering old shows and films can be done faster and better.

Animation:

AI helps automate tedious frame-by-frame work, assists in motion capture cleanups, and even predicts how characters should move based on style and emotion.

Basically, AI is giving artists superpowers. Less time fixing hair strands, more time creating epic dragon battles.

Journalism and AI: News by Neural Networks

Believe it or not, a lot of news articles you read today — especially quick financial summaries, sports recaps, and weather updates — might be penned (or keyboard-smashed) by AI.

Automated Journalism:

Outlets like The Associated Press and Reuters use AI to produce thousands of short, factual articles at lightning speed.

AI in Content Curation:

News apps and platforms use AI to personalize what articles you see, based on your reading habits.

While some fear that AI will "replace journalists," the smarter take is: it frees up human reporters to focus on deep investigative stories — the real heart of journalism.

AI-Generated Art and Virtual Influencers

This one's so wild it deserves its own shoutout.

AI Art:

Thanks to models like DALL·E and Midjourney, artists are blending human creativity with machine imagination to create album covers, book illustrations, movie posters, and more.

Virtual Influencers:

Instagram personalities like Lil Miquela (who looks completely real but is 100% virtual) are AI-crafted brands raking in sponsorships.

Yes, brands are paying computer-generated models real money. Welcome to the future.

Challenges and Criticisms

Of course, not everything is rainbows and robot unicorns.

Originality:

Critics argue that AI-generated content can sometimes feel hollow or derivative — because it is trained on existing human creations.

Ethics and Copyright:

Who owns AI-generated songs, images, or stories? The programmer? The user? The AI itself? (Plot twist: the answer's still fuzzy.)

Job Displacement:

Artists, writers, musicians, and media workers worry about being undercut by faster, cheaper AI alternatives.

These are real concerns, and as AI fans (and creators), we have a responsibility to advocate for fair use, credit, and human-AI collaboration — not exploitation.

Wrapping It Up

AI in entertainment and media is like a rock band made up of humans and robots jamming together. Sometimes they create pure magic, sometimes the guitar catches fire, but either way, the show must go on.

If we play it right, AI won't replace creativity — it'll amplify it, opening up wild new possibilities for stories, music, art, and beyond.

And hey, if someday my autobiography is co-written by an AI and turned into a blockbuster movie starring a hologram of me riding a laser shark... honestly? I'll take it.

9.2 AI for Education and Content Creation

If there's one area where AI is truly leveling up human potential, it's education and content creation. I mean, think about it: not only can AI now help you ace that online test you've been avoiding (no judgment), but it's also creating an entire universe of content with a snap of your fingers. Whether it's generating lesson plans, designing creative writing prompts, or composing an entire research paper — AI is making things way easier.

Now, if you're thinking AI in education is like the Terminator showing up to teach your Algebra 101 class, don't worry! We're not talking about that kind of disruption. AI is more like the best teaching assistant you could have — helping with research, offering feedback, and even encouraging creativity. But don't just take my word for it — let's dive into how AI is shaping education and content creation for the better.

AI in Education: The Future of Learning

Okay, let's get one thing straight: AI is not here to replace teachers (we're not living in The Matrix... yet). Instead, it's here to be the ultimate sidekick — a super-powered, never-tired teaching assistant who's available 24/7. Imagine having a tutor that doesn't need coffee breaks and never gives up on explaining fractions (thank you, AI).

Personalized Learning

One of the most exciting applications of AI in education is personalized learning. Everyone learns differently, and AI can assess a student's strengths, weaknesses, and learning style to craft individualized lessons. For example, platforms like Khan Academy and Duolingo use AI to adapt their courses based on your performance, tailoring the difficulty of lessons to match your pace. No more falling behind because of a one-size-fits-all approach!

Intelligent Tutoring Systems

AI-powered tutoring systems are like having a private tutor who doesn't need to charge by the hour. Tools like Socratic (from Google) help students by answering questions in real time, guiding them through math problems, essays, or science concepts. These systems can break things down into digestible steps, helping students understand even the most difficult subjects.

Grading and Feedback

Teachers are superheroes, but let's face it: grading papers, providing feedback, and managing assignments can be exhausting. AI can handle the repetitive work, giving teachers more time to focus on creative lesson planning and one-on-one interaction with students. AI-powered platforms can quickly grade assignments, give instant feedback on essays, and help students revise their work for better grades.

Automating Administrative Tasks

AI isn't just helping in the classroom — it's also streamlining school administration. From tracking student performance to scheduling classes, AI tools like IBM Watson Education help schools make data-driven decisions to improve learning outcomes. By automating these back-end processes, educational institutions can save time and resources.

AI in Content Creation: The Ultimate Creative Partner

Now that we've covered how AI is transforming the classroom, let's talk about how it's shaking things up in the content creation world. Whether you're a writer, musician, designer, or marketer, AI is like having a creative assistant who's got your back 24/7. It's here to take your content game from "meh" to "wow!" faster than you can say "content strategy."

Writing and Copy Creation

AI's big claim to fame in content creation is its ability to generate written content. Tools like GPT-3 and Jasper (formerly Jarvis) are already helping marketers, bloggers, and even novelists generate articles, blog posts, marketing copy, and more in seconds. You give it a prompt — and it gives you paragraphs of well-structured text.
Sure, you might have to do some tweaking here and there, but for those "I'm stuck" moments, AI is a lifesaver. Think of it as your trusty creative partner who's always got an idea brewing.

Design and Visual Content

AI isn't just about words — it's got the visual arts covered too. Tools like DALL·E 2 and Midjourney can turn text descriptions into high-quality images, illustrations, or even logos.

Just type something like, "A futuristic city at sunset," and boom — you get a stunning image in seconds.

AI-powered design tools, such as Canva's Magic Write, also offer text-to-image functionalities, helping businesses and creators craft professional-looking graphics without needing an advanced design background. Want to make an eye-catching social media post? You're covered.

Music and Audio Production

Let's talk tunes. AI can generate music for podcasts, videos, and even commercials. Amper Music, AIVA, and Jukedeck allow you to create music in any genre, all driven by AI algorithms that analyze the emotions and tone of your content. If you're working on a YouTube video and need the perfect background track, AI can generate it for you.

Even more fun? AI is also able to remix and alter existing music. So if you're feeling creative and want to throw a pop song into a jazz remix, or add a hip-hop twist to a classical piece, AI's got your back.

Video and Animation

Creating videos and animations can be time-consuming, especially if you don't have a full production crew at your disposal. Thankfully, AI tools like Runway and Synthesia allow creators to produce high-quality video content with ease.

For instance, Synthesia can generate entire videos with AI-powered avatars that speak in multiple languages — perfect for training videos or social media content.

Ethical Considerations in AI-Powered Education and Content Creation

While AI is a fantastic tool for learning and content creation, we can't ignore the ethical concerns that come along with its use. From concerns about privacy to bias in AI-generated content, it's essential to have conversations about the implications of using these tools. For instance, if students are using AI to generate essays, are they actually learning the material? And when AI is used to create content, how do we ensure that it doesn't propagate harmful stereotypes or misinformation?

Ethical AI usage requires responsibility from both developers and users, ensuring that these tools are used in ways that promote fairness, accuracy, and creativity.

The Future of AI in Education and Content Creation

Looking ahead, it's clear that AI is only going to become more integrated into both education and content creation. For education, we can expect more intelligent systems that provide real-time feedback, even more personalized learning paths, and stronger AI-tutoring systems that support both students and teachers. For content creators, AI will continue to push the boundaries of what's possible — whether it's writing, designing, or even composing.

AI isn't about replacing the human touch — it's about empowering individuals and helping them unleash their full potential. Whether you're a teacher, student, writer, or artist, the future is bright, and AI is here to make the journey a little bit smoother. Just remember — don't let your AI-powered assistant take all the credit for that perfect paper or masterpiece. You still deserve some applause.

9.3 Generative AI in Business and Marketing

If you had told me five years ago that AI would soon be running marketing campaigns, designing logos, writing blog posts, and optimizing ad targeting in real time, I would've looked at you like you'd just proposed training a goldfish to run a startup. But, here we are, in 2025, and guess what? AI is doing all that—and it's doing it so well, some businesses are questioning if they need human employees at all. (Okay, maybe not quite that extreme... but you get the point.)

Generative AI is shaking up business operations and marketing strategies faster than a caffeinated intern trying to meet a deadline. In the past, marketing departments were stuck relying on traditional methods: focus groups, market research, brainstorming sessions, and all that jazz. While those methods still have their place, AI has transformed the marketing game by automating, optimizing, and even predicting consumer behavior with precision that humans simply can't match. Ready to dive into how AI is changing business and marketing? Let's get into it!

AI in Business: Operational Efficiency and Innovation

AI is no longer just a "cool tech" used by massive corporations — it's a necessity for modern businesses looking to stay competitive. From streamlining operations to helping businesses make smarter decisions, AI is the behind-the-scenes force powering many of today's most successful organizations.

Automating Repetitive Tasks

Let's face it: there's a lot of boring, repetitive stuff we all do at work. The endless number-crunching, scheduling, managing emails, and sorting through customer data can feel like you're drowning in a sea of admin. But guess what? AI is here to throw you a lifeline. Tools like UiPath and Automation Anywhere are streamlining business processes by automating routine tasks, allowing employees to focus on higher-value work. Want to automate inventory management, customer support inquiries, or invoicing? AI can handle that.

Predictive Analytics for Better Decision-Making

If you're making business decisions based on gut instinct alone, you're in trouble. AI has changed the way companies approach decision-making by using predictive analytics. These algorithms analyze vast amounts of historical data, customer behavior, market trends, and external factors to predict future outcomes with incredible accuracy. Whether it's forecasting sales, understanding customer churn, or predicting inventory needs, AI helps businesses make smarter, data-driven decisions in real-time. Think of it as your crystal ball—except, you know, way more reliable.

AI-Powered Personalization

Customers today expect personalized experiences. Gone are the days of "one-size-fits-all" marketing. With the help of AI, businesses can now create hyper-targeted ads, product recommendations, and content that feels tailored to each individual customer's preferences. Machine learning algorithms can track user behavior across websites, social media, and emails, and use this data to predict the best time, product, and messaging for each customer. Companies like Netflix, Spotify, and Amazon have mastered the art of AI-driven personalization — and if you've ever found yourself endlessly binge-watching a show or buying more stuff you don't need, you can thank AI for that.

AI in Marketing: Creating Content, Optimizing Campaigns, and Scaling Success

Marketing is where AI truly shines. Gone are the days of manually sorting through data or creating content by hand (well, almost). AI is making marketing faster, more efficient, and ultimately more profitable. The best part? It's helping marketers create content that resonates with consumers on a whole new level.

AI-Generated Content

You probably already know that AI can generate text (hello, GPT-3), but did you know it can also generate product descriptions, blog posts, ad copy, email campaigns, and more? For marketers with tight deadlines or heavy workloads, AI-powered writing assistants like Jasper (formerly Jarvis) can create high-quality content in minutes. Want to whip up a blog post about "The Future of AI in Marketing"? Just type in a few keywords, and bam — you've got a draft.

Chatbots and Virtual Assistants

AI-powered chatbots are revolutionizing customer service and sales. You've probably chatted with a chatbot when you had an issue with an online order or needed quick help on a website. These bots can resolve a surprising amount of problems, 24/7, without ever needing to take a coffee break. Brands like Sephora and H&M use AI chatbots to guide customers through the buying process, answer FAQs, and even recommend products. A chatbot's job isn't just to make customers happy — it's also gathering valuable data for businesses to analyze.

Ad Optimization

AI isn't just automating ad creation (although it's doing that too) — it's also optimizing ads in real-time. Gone are the days of launching a campaign, crossing your fingers, and hoping for the best. AI tools like Google Ads and Facebook's AI algorithms analyze thousands of variables to optimize ad targeting, timing, and placement. In simple terms, AI can tell you exactly when to show an ad, to whom, and with what messaging to maximize engagement. It's like having a super-efficient marketing guru working for you, minus the huge salary.

Generative AI in Business and Marketing: A Game Changer

While we've already established that AI is transforming various facets of business and marketing, what sets generative AI apart is its ability to create content, products, and ideas from scratch — making it a game-changer for companies looking to innovate.

Product Design and Prototyping

Generative AI can design new products, services, and experiences with just a few inputs from human creators. Generative design software (like Autodesk's Generative Design Tool) allows engineers and designers to input basic parameters (size, material, strength, etc.), and the AI system will generate hundreds — sometimes thousands — of design alternatives. This process drastically speeds up product design, enabling businesses to find optimal solutions faster and cheaper. Think about how AI might help design the next-gen sneakers or the perfect ergonomic office chair.

Marketing Campaigns That Write Themselves

When it comes to generative AI in marketing, imagine an AI system that can not only create individual pieces of content but entire marketing campaigns. Some platforms now use AI to generate an entire marketing strategy based on specific inputs like audience, goals, and budget. From crafting copy and designing visuals to optimizing social media posts, generative AI is streamlining the campaign creation process from start to finish. It's like having a marketing agency in your pocket (and no, they don't charge an arm and a leg).

Visual Content Creation

If you've ever struggled with coming up with visual assets for your brand, you're not alone. But now, AI-powered platforms like DALL·E or MidJourney are making it easy to generate unique images and graphics from simple text prompts. Need a futuristic cityscape to showcase your new tech product? Just ask the AI, and watch it deliver. This is a huge time-saver for businesses that need high-quality visuals without hiring a designer or photographer.

Wrapping It Up: AI for Business and Marketing Is Just Getting Started

If you're still skeptical about the role of AI in business and marketing, I get it — the idea of machines running our operations can feel like we're heading toward Skynet territory. But in reality, AI is here to enhance creativity, increase efficiency, and help businesses thrive in an ever-evolving digital landscape.

From streamlining operations and automating tasks to crafting personalized marketing campaigns and generating content, generative AI is becoming an essential tool for success in 2025 and beyond. Whether you're running a small business or leading a global corporation, embracing AI can help you stay ahead of the competition — and maybe even put that "AI-powered assistant" on your resume. So buckle up, because AI is here to stay, and it's only going to make your business smarter, faster, and more creative.

9.4 Healthcare and Scientific Discovery with AI

If there's one industry that's experiencing a renaissance thanks to AI, it's healthcare. Imagine AI acting as a super-sleuth detective, zooming through endless data to find patterns that doctors and scientists might miss. Or picture AI working as a hyper-efficient assistant, taking care of the tedious tasks so that healthcare professionals can focus on providing better care. It's like the ultimate medical sidekick — and it's only getting started.

The truth is, AI is already playing a huge role in both healthcare and scientific research, from diagnosing diseases earlier than ever before to unlocking new pathways for treatments that could change the world. We're talking about AI transforming not just the way we heal, but how we discover new cures, understand the human body, and fight diseases that have eluded us for centuries. Intrigued? Well, buckle up, because AI's impact on healthcare and scientific discovery is nothing short of revolutionary.

AI in Healthcare: Revolutionizing Diagnosis and Treatment

Healthcare is a field where precision is literally a matter of life and death, and that's where AI shines the brightest. By processing vast amounts of medical data, analyzing images, and predicting outcomes, AI is already improving the quality of care that patients receive and saving lives in the process.

Early Disease Detection

One of the biggest breakthroughs AI brings to healthcare is its ability to detect diseases early, sometimes even before symptoms appear. AI systems are particularly good at analyzing medical imaging (like X-rays, CT scans, and MRIs) and finding patterns that human doctors may overlook. For example, AI tools like Google Health's AI have shown the ability to detect breast cancer with greater accuracy than human radiologists. And it's not just cancer. AI is helping doctors diagnose everything from diabetic retinopathy to early-stage Alzheimer's disease, giving patients a fighting chance before things worsen.

Precision Medicine

Thanks to machine learning, doctors now have a new tool for offering personalized treatment plans for patients. Rather than following a generic one-size-fits-all approach, AI allows for precision medicine, where treatments are tailored based on a patient's genetic makeup, lifestyle, and environmental factors. With this level of customization, patients can receive treatments that are much more likely to be effective, with fewer side effects. The potential is vast — from using AI to predict which cancer treatment will work best for a patient to customizing drug dosages for someone based on their genetic code. This is the future of medicine, and it's happening right now.

Robotic Surgery

Let's talk about AI-powered robotic surgery. AI is enabling robots to perform complex surgeries with incredible precision. No, we're not talking about a robot with a scalpel wandering around the OR — these are advanced systems that assist human surgeons by offering enhanced accuracy, reducing human error, and improving recovery times. Take Da Vinci Surgical Systems, for example. These robots allow surgeons to perform minimally invasive procedures through small incisions, leading to faster recovery, less pain, and fewer complications for patients. The result? Patients benefit from both human expertise and AI-driven precision.

AI in Drug Discovery

The process of discovering new drugs is long, expensive, and full of trial and error. But guess what? AI is speeding up the entire process. By analyzing massive datasets, AI models can identify potential drug candidates much faster than traditional methods. Companies like Atomwise are using AI to search for new molecules that could treat diseases like cancer and Ebola. AI's ability to simulate the effects of drugs on the human body means we can predict which compounds are more likely to succeed in clinical trials, thus cutting down on development costs and time. It's a game-changer for pharmaceutical companies and could lead to life-saving medications reaching the market quicker.

Scientific Discovery: Accelerating Breakthroughs

Healthcare isn't the only field where AI is making waves. When it comes to scientific discovery, AI is serving as a high-powered engine that accelerates research, helps scientists analyze complex data, and even generates new hypotheses.

Advancing Research with AI Models

In scientific research, AI is being used to process massive datasets from experiments that would take humans years to analyze. Whether it's genomic data, astronomical observations, or climate models, AI allows scientists to extract insights and uncover patterns much faster than traditional methods. For example, AI is being used in genomics to analyze sequences of DNA, helping researchers understand the genetic basis of diseases and find new targets for drugs. This has led to gene-editing advances (like CRISPR) that could potentially cure genetic disorders in the near future.

AI in Drug Repurposing

AI's ability to analyze large sets of data also plays a major role in drug repurposing, which involves finding new uses for existing medications. Researchers have already used AI to identify drugs that could work against diseases like COVID-19 or Parkinson's disease. AI's ability to sift through reams of existing data, clinical trial results, and molecular information makes it an invaluable tool in the search for new treatment options. Insilico Medicine, for example, uses AI to accelerate the discovery of novel drug candidates and identify those that could work for diseases that currently have no effective treatments.

Climate Change and Environmental Research

AI is also having a profound impact on environmental science. From predicting the impacts of climate change to monitoring deforestation and pollution, AI is helping scientists understand our planet and how to protect it. For instance, DeepMind, Google's AI division, is working on using AI to predict energy consumption patterns, enabling more efficient use of resources. Researchers are also using AI models to predict how ecosystems will change due to global warming, giving us a chance to prepare for potential environmental disasters. AI is helping us understand the world around us in ways that were once thought impossible.

The Ethical Dilemma: AI in Healthcare and Scientific Research

As much as AI is revolutionizing healthcare and scientific research, it comes with its own set of ethical challenges. In healthcare, the privacy of patient data is a major concern. How do we protect sensitive information when AI systems are analyzing vast amounts of personal data? Additionally, there's the risk of algorithmic bias. If an AI system is trained on biased data, it could make decisions that are unfair or discriminatory — something we've already seen in certain healthcare AI applications.

In scientific research, there's the question of responsibility: Who is accountable if an AI system suggests a wrong course of treatment or makes a flawed discovery? As AI takes on more critical roles in both healthcare and science, it's crucial that we put safeguards in place to ensure that the technology is used ethically, responsibly, and with transparency.

The Future of AI in Healthcare and Science

Looking ahead, the role of AI in healthcare and scientific research will only grow. As AI technology becomes more advanced, we'll likely see even faster medical breakthroughs, more efficient treatments, and improved patient outcomes. AI may even help us solve some of humanity's biggest problems, from curing previously untreatable diseases to mitigating the effects of climate change.

But while the future is exciting, it's important to remember that AI in healthcare and science is a tool — a powerful one, yes, but a tool nonetheless. It will never replace the need for human judgment, compassion, and oversight. However, when used ethically and responsibly, AI will continue to serve as an invaluable partner in our quest to better understand and improve the world of health and science.

So, here's to AI — the unsung hero in healthcare and scientific discovery, working tirelessly in the background, making our lives better, and potentially saving us all from things we've yet to imagine.

9.5 Interactive Applications (Games, Chatbots, AR/VR)

Imagine you're playing a video game where the enemies don't follow pre-programmed routines but adapt to your every move, creating an experience that feels different every time. Or you're having a conversation with a chatbot that understands not just the words you say, but the emotions behind them. Or even better, you're exploring a digital world through augmented reality (AR) or virtual reality (VR), where the lines between the real world and digital creations blur. Welcome to the fascinating universe of interactive applications, where Generative AI is setting the stage for the next big leap in how we experience the digital world.

Whether it's enhancing video games with more intelligent NPCs (Non-Player Characters), creating realistic conversational agents, or transforming how we interact with digital spaces, generative AI is revolutionizing interactivity. Games are no longer just about players following scripted narratives; they're about creating personalized, dynamic experiences. Chatbots aren't just responding with preset answers, they're learning, adapting, and providing more nuanced, lifelike interactions. And AR/VR? Well, with AI generating more immersive and interactive worlds, you're in for a ride that feels straight out of science fiction.

AI in Gaming: Dynamic, Personalized Experiences

The gaming industry has always been a pioneer in embracing technology, and AI is taking it to the next level. Imagine playing your favorite video game, but this time, the characters in the game aren't just mindlessly following a script. They react to your actions, adapt to your strategies, and learn from your decisions. This is the promise of AI-powered dynamic gaming experiences.

AI-Powered NPCs

In traditional games, non-player characters (NPCs) follow pre-determined paths, with predictable reactions. While this works for basic games, Generative AI introduces a new level of interaction. Now, NPCs can become more autonomous, creating unscripted, reactive behaviors based on the player's actions. This means that NPCs can evolve, develop strategies, and offer a much more engaging challenge to players. Take games like The Elder Scrolls V: Skyrim or Red Dead Redemption 2 as examples. With AI-driven character behavior, NPCs can act in a more lifelike way, resulting in a richer, more immersive gaming experience. Whether it's their dialogue or the way they respond to your choices, the interaction feels a lot more personal.

Procedural Content Generation

Another exciting use of AI in gaming is procedural content generation. Instead of developers manually designing every level, AI can create infinite variations of environments, missions, and scenarios. Think about it — in games like Minecraft or No Man's Sky, the virtual worlds are vast and nearly limitless. With the power of generative AI, games can automatically generate new environments, characters, and even quests on the fly, ensuring that players never run out of things to explore. This keeps the experience fresh and exciting, no matter how much time you've spent in the game.

Personalized Gaming Experiences

Not all players play games the same way. Some might focus on storylines, others on exploration, and some on combat. AI can take these preferences into account and tailor the game experience for each individual player. Imagine an AI that adjusts the difficulty based on how well you're doing, or a game that changes its narrative arc based on the choices you make. This personalized touch could make every gaming session feel unique and deeply connected to your style.

Chatbots and Virtual Assistants: Conversations That Feel Real

We've all used chatbots at some point, whether to troubleshoot a product or get some customer service. But let's be honest — most chatbots still sound like they've been trained on a script written by a robot (and not the cool kind of robot). Thanks to Generative AI, this is changing fast. Today's chatbots are evolving from rigid, rule-based systems to more dynamic, intelligent conversational agents.

Conversational AI: Beyond Simple Responses

Generative AI has significantly improved the ability of chatbots to understand context, maintain conversations, and even respond with emotional intelligence. For example, AI models like GPT or BERT can generate responses that feel natural, nuanced, and appropriate based on the tone of the conversation. Rather than a chatbot simply answering "yes" or "no" to your inquiries, these advanced systems can carry on longer conversations, understand subtle hints, and even adapt their responses based on your mood or tone.

For example, if you ask a chatbot about a product, it can not only answer your question but also provide recommendations based on your preferences, past purchases, or even help you troubleshoot problems in a conversational manner. It's like talking to a knowledgeable friend who's always ready to assist.

Chatbots in Customer Service

When it comes to customer service, chatbots with Generative AI can make a huge impact. By understanding natural language and learning from past interactions, AI-powered chatbots can respond to customer inquiries much faster and more accurately than traditional systems. Whether you're asking about your bank balance, tracking a package, or looking for troubleshooting help, these intelligent chatbots can resolve your issue faster and provide better satisfaction. And with constant learning, these bots get better over time, handling increasingly complex questions and scenarios.

Augmented Reality (AR) & Virtual Reality (VR): Immersive Worlds Powered by AI

The future of gaming, entertainment, education, and even workplace training lies in augmented reality (AR) and virtual reality (VR). These technologies are already opening up exciting new ways to experience the world around us, and when paired with Generative AI, they can deliver experiences that are even more dynamic and immersive.

AR: Blending Digital with the Real World

Imagine walking through a museum, and as you stand in front of a painting, your AR headset displays information about the artist, their techniques, and even virtual versions of the painting coming to life. With AI-powered AR, this kind of experience is becoming possible. The ability to generate real-time interactive digital content based on your location, movements, or objects in your environment is changing how we perceive the world. AR apps can adjust the digital content dynamically based on the user's actions or surroundings, providing highly personalized and immersive experiences. For instance, apps like Pokemon GO or IKEA Place already use AR to enhance user interaction, and Generative AI will only make these experiences richer.

VR: Creating Entirely New Realities

Virtual Reality is about immersion. It's about leaving the real world behind and diving into an entirely new digital realm. When combined with AI, VR can generate more realistic and engaging worlds that evolve as you interact with them. Whether it's a VR game where the environment changes based on your actions or a virtual tour where AI tailors the experience to your interests, the possibilities are endless. AI-driven VR can create more fluid, adaptive, and lifelike virtual environments that don't just react to your movements but anticipate them, adding depth and realism.

The Future of Interactive AI

Looking ahead, AI-powered interactive applications are set to redefine how we experience the digital world. From gaming to communication, from customer service to AR/VR, AI is making everything smarter, more dynamic, and increasingly personalized. With its ability to learn, adapt, and create, generative AI is driving the next wave of innovation in interactive applications. And this is just the beginning. As technology advances, we can expect even more exciting developments, from hyper-realistic games that evolve based on your personal style to chatbots that are indistinguishable from human conversation.

Interactive AI is here to stay, and it's about to get a whole lot more interesting. So whether you're exploring new worlds in VR, chatting with a bot that's almost like a friend, or playing a game that's different every time you load it up, one thing is certain — with AI, the digital world just became a whole lot more interactive.

Chapter 10: The Road Ahead in Generative AI

Cue the dramatic music. You've battled code errors, tamed neural nets, and generated a questionable number of cat images. Now what? This final chapter is where we stare boldly into the future—cue wind blowing through digital hair.

Here, we address the limitations of current generative AI models, explore potential breakthroughs, and discuss the broader societal impacts of AI proliferation. Topics include ethics, regulation, job opportunities, and the importance of continuous learning. It's both a reflection and a roadmap, guiding you from beginner to future expert.

10.1 Limitations of Today's Generative AI

Generative AI is undoubtedly one of the most exciting and transformative fields in technology today. From creating realistic images and videos to writing compelling stories and composing music, the possibilities seem endless. But before you start dreaming of a future where AI does everything for us, it's essential to understand that the technology still has some big gaps to fill. As with any breakthrough technology, there are limitations we need to be aware of.

Let's get one thing straight — Generative AI is amazing, but it's far from perfect. While it can create beautiful images or generate coherent text, it can't always produce the level of consistency, accuracy, and creativity that we humans can. It might sound like I'm downplaying its potential, but I promise you, I'm not. The reality is that there are still a lot of hurdles to overcome before AI reaches its full potential. But hey, that's the fun part of being on the cutting edge of technology, right?

1. Lack of True Understanding

One of the fundamental limitations of current generative AI models is their lack of true understanding. While these models can produce text, images, or even music that appear intelligent, they don't truly understand the meaning behind what they generate. Think about it: when you ask a Generative AI to write a story or generate a paragraph, it uses patterns in the data it's been trained on to produce something that fits. But unlike humans, it doesn't have an inherent understanding of what the story is about or the emotional depth of the content. It's essentially mimicking intelligence without comprehending the world. So while the output can look great, don't expect the AI to "get" the deeper meaning or complexities of what it's generating.

This lack of true comprehension also means that AI can easily get things wrong. Imagine asking an AI to summarize a highly complex scientific article. The result may seem plausible on the surface, but it may lack important nuances, miss key details, or even make factual errors. The AI isn't actively thinking about the material in the way a human expert would — it's simply predicting the most likely output based on patterns.

2. Creativity and Innovation – Still Human Territory

While generative AI can mimic and create from the vast pool of data it's been trained on, its ability to truly innovate and come up with groundbreaking ideas is still limited. When it comes to creativity, AI models are more like brilliant copycats rather than pioneers. They can remix, rearrange, and recombine existing ideas, but they're not equipped to come up with something entirely new or radically different on their own.

For example, an AI model trained on thousands of pieces of art can generate beautiful paintings in various styles. But can it create a whole new genre of art that hasn't been seen before? Probably not. It lacks the deep understanding of cultural shifts, personal experiences, and emotional depth that humans bring to the creative process. So, as much as we might want AI to replace our writers, artists, and musicians, there's a certain spark of human ingenuity and intuition that AI can't replicate (yet).

3. Bias and Ethical Concerns

This is a huge issue in the world of AI today. Generative AI models learn from data, and as we know, data can be inherently biased. This means that when AI is trained on biased datasets (which is often the case), the resulting output can also reflect these biases. This could be in the form of gender, racial, or even ideological biases that show up in the generated content.

For instance, an AI trained on biased data might produce stereotypical or discriminatory content, or it may reinforce harmful societal views without any awareness. This has already been seen in some generative models that produce problematic or offensive text when prompted in certain ways. There's also the risk of deepfakes—manipulated images or videos that can distort reality and cause harm by spreading misinformation.

AI developers and researchers are working hard to mitigate these risks by designing algorithms that identify and reduce bias. However, this remains an ongoing challenge, and ethical considerations will need to play a central role as generative AI continues to evolve.

4. Data and Training Dependency

Generative AI is entirely dependent on the data it's been trained on. This means that the quality and diversity of the data it's exposed to directly impact its performance. If an AI model is trained on a narrow or biased dataset, it can only generate outputs based on that information. It's like teaching a student from a textbook that's missing crucial chapters — the output will be incomplete or skewed.

Additionally, AI needs massive amounts of computational resources to train on this vast amount of data. This makes it expensive and energy-intensive. For smaller developers or those with limited access to powerful computing resources, training generative AI models can be a significant barrier to entry. This also contributes to the environmental footprint of AI, which is a growing concern.

5. Generalization – Stuck in the Narrow Lane

Another limitation is that current generative AI models excel in narrow tasks but struggle with generalization. For example, an AI trained to generate realistic images might do a fantastic job with landscapes but fail miserably when tasked with generating a coherent human face. Similarly, an AI trained to generate text might excel at writing poems but falter when asked to generate technical manuals or legal documents.

This is where the distinction between Narrow AI and General AI becomes important. Narrow AI, which is what we have today, is highly specialized and excels in specific domains. However, it can't handle the broad, multifaceted problem-solving that General AI would. So while your AI might ace writing a story, don't ask it to manage your day-to-day tasks or solve an engineering problem. It's still very narrow in its capabilities.

6. Real-Time Adaptation – AI's Struggle with Real-World Complexity

In many situations, AI models perform well when given static data — like a pre-recorded image or a well-defined text prompt. However, real-world scenarios are dynamic, and AI models struggle to keep up with constant changes and unpredictability. Imagine asking an AI to help you navigate through a crowded street during rush hour or suggesting solutions in a fast-changing business environment. In these contexts, the AI can't adapt quickly enough, especially if it hasn't been trained on such complex, constantly changing data.

This is why AI is still limited when it comes to tasks that require ongoing real-time decision-making or improvised solutions. The models can struggle to analyze live data as it changes or to understand complex, unforeseen circumstances.

7. The Black Box Problem

AI is often referred to as a "black box" because it's difficult to understand how or why it generates the outputs it does. This is especially true for highly complex models like Generative Adversarial Networks (GANs) or Transformer-based models. Sure, they might produce great results, but trying to figure out exactly why they made a specific decision is often a mystery.

This lack of transparency is a significant issue, especially when it comes to accountability. If an AI generates a biased or harmful piece of content, it can be challenging to pinpoint why it happened or how to prevent it from happening again. The black box problem raises concerns, particularly in critical areas like healthcare, legal decisions, or finance, where explainability is crucial.

Generative AI is an impressive technology, but it's still in its infancy, with several limitations holding it back from reaching its full potential. The lack of true understanding, the inability to create truly innovative ideas, biases in the training data, and dependency on massive datasets are just a few of the challenges AI faces today. However, as the technology continues to advance, these limitations are being actively addressed. So, while AI can't do everything just yet, its trajectory is incredibly promising. It's just a matter of time before it overcomes these hurdles and transforms industries in ways we can only dream of today.

So, while AI may not be able to write your novel or paint your masterpiece quite as you would, it's getting closer to that point every day. Until then, let's continue to work alongside AI, embrace its strengths, and keep pushing the boundaries of what's possible. After all, we're all in this together.

10.2 Societal Impacts and Opportunities

Generative AI isn't just a technological breakthrough; it's a societal revolution waiting to unfold. If you've been living under a rock (or perhaps you've been busy binge-watching TV shows), you may not have noticed the AI-powered world taking over everything from art to education, and even healthcare. But don't worry — that's exactly why we're here.

To explore how these emerging technologies are poised to change the way we live, work, and think. Trust me, the future is going to be both exciting and a bit wild.

The impact of generative AI on society isn't just about robots writing novels or machines making art. It's about how we interact with each other, how businesses operate, and how we solve complex global challenges. Let's break it down: On one hand, AI promises to increase productivity, create new jobs, and democratize knowledge. On the other hand, it also raises questions about automation, privacy, ethics, and equity. Will we use this powerful tool to enhance human potential, or will it further entrench existing inequalities? Spoiler alert: it's up to us how we shape this future.

1. Job Automation and the Future of Work

One of the most discussed topics when it comes to AI is automation. If you're worried about robots stealing your job, you're not alone. Generative AI, with its ability to generate text, images, and even video content, has the potential to automate many tasks that were once considered uniquely human. We're talking about everything from customer service to content creation, marketing campaigns, and even software coding.

While this sounds like the end of the world as we know it, it's actually a mixed bag. On one hand, automation can drastically improve efficiency and productivity. Imagine businesses running like clockwork with AI handling repetitive tasks. On the other hand, AI also raises the fear of job displacement, especially in sectors like manufacturing, retail, and even creative industries.

However, it's not all doom and gloom. History shows that technological advancements often create new jobs, industries, and opportunities, even if they displace some existing roles. In fact, as AI takes over more repetitive tasks, humans can focus on tasks requiring creativity, emotional intelligence, and complex decision-making. This shift could lead to an evolution of the workforce, where humans and AI work together to drive innovation. The trick, of course, is ensuring that displaced workers have the skills and support they need to adapt to these changes.

2. Education and Access to Knowledge

Generative AI is also reshaping education. Gone are the days when learning was limited to textbooks and a set curriculum. Today, AI can create personalized learning experiences tailored to an individual's strengths, weaknesses, and interests. For example, AI-powered tutors can assist students with their homework, explain concepts in ways that make sense to them, and help them learn at their own pace.

But the potential goes beyond personalized education. AI models can automatically generate educational materials in multiple languages, breaking down barriers to access. Imagine a world where anyone, anywhere, could receive quality education at little to no cost. Whether you're in a remote village in Africa or a bustling city in Asia, generative AI could give you access to top-tier learning materials, making education far more democratic.

In addition, generative AI has the potential to revolutionize content creation, helping teachers create custom lesson plans, videos, and simulations without needing to spend hours putting them together. This would give educators more time to focus on interactive, high-level teaching. Of course, we need to make sure that the AI-generated content is accurate, non-biased, and culturally relevant to all learners, but the possibilities are truly transformative.

3. Healthcare and Medicine

When it comes to healthcare, the impact of generative AI could be absolutely life-changing. AI models can already analyze medical data, assist in drug discovery, and help physicians diagnose diseases with incredible accuracy. But the next frontier is generative AI: Imagine AI helping to design personalized treatments or generating synthetic medical data to assist in the development of new drugs or therapies. AI could even help generate simulations for surgeries, allowing medical professionals to practice in virtual environments before performing real-life procedures.

The potential for AI to assist in healthcare is not just about improving patient outcomes but also about making healthcare more accessible and affordable. With generative AI, we could see the development of more efficient and tailored healthcare systems that can help diagnose patients faster, generate treatment options more precisely, and even design medical devices suited to the individual.

However, this opportunity is not without risks. Issues of privacy, data security, and ethical considerations in using AI in healthcare will need to be carefully addressed. Patients must trust that their medical data is used ethically, and AI models must be transparent and accountable for their decisions.

4. Ethical Considerations and Bias

Generative AI brings a world of opportunities, but it also comes with significant ethical challenges. For example, AI systems can amplify biases if they are trained on biased datasets. This can lead to discrimination in critical areas like hiring, law enforcement, healthcare, and more. While the technology can be groundbreaking, we need to ensure that it's used fairly, with ethical guidelines to prevent harm to vulnerable groups.

This issue is particularly important in sectors like criminal justice, where AI tools are being used to predict recidivism or assist in sentencing. If these models are biased, they can perpetuate racial or socioeconomic disparities. As generative AI becomes more embedded in our daily lives, it's essential for companies, governments, and researchers to establish clear ethical frameworks to guide its use. This includes transparency, fairness, accountability, and responsibility for AI's actions.

5. AI for Social Good

The flipside of these challenges is the potential for AI to create tremendous social good. Generative AI can help tackle some of the world's most pressing problems, such as climate change, poverty, and global health crises. For instance, AI can help generate solutions for renewable energy or simulate climate models to predict the impacts of global warming.

Similarly, AI could be used to generate synthetic data to study the effects of social policies or develop new methods for alleviating hunger and poverty. By using AI to analyze and predict solutions, humanity could solve some of the most complex global challenges. It's about harnessing the power of AI ethically and creatively to improve the human condition.

Conclusion: Embracing the Future

The societal impacts of generative AI are profound, and the opportunities are endless. As we move toward an AI-powered future, we must ensure that we embrace these technologies thoughtfully, balancing progress with responsibility. We have the chance to use AI to enhance our lives, create new industries, solve global challenges, and make the world a better place for future generations. But to do this, we must be mindful of the risks, work to mitigate bias, and make sure the benefits are accessible to everyone.

Generative AI is not something to fear. It's something to explore and shape, ensuring that it remains a tool for positive change. The future is what we make of it — and with generative AI, the possibilities are truly limitless. So buckle up, folks. The AI revolution has just begun, and we're all part of it.

10.3 The Role of Regulation and Ethics

Ah, regulation—the word that often makes people groan and roll their eyes, especially in the fast-moving world of technology. But before you start daydreaming about yet another bureaucratic mess, let's talk about why regulation and ethics in the realm of generative AI are crucial, and why we can't just let this powerful tech run wild like a robot on roller skates. Imagine if AI could autonomously create everything from news articles to realistic deepfakes. If left unchecked, the potential for misuse, bias, and harm would be enormous. It's like giving a toddler the keys to a car—dangerous, unpredictable, and very much in need of supervision.

Generative AI holds immense power to shape our world, but with great power comes great responsibility. So, while we all love the shiny new toy that is AI, we also need to ensure it doesn't turn into an uncontrollable monster. How do we make sure it serves humanity rather than causing chaos? Enter regulation—the not-so-glamorous but absolutely necessary foundation that will guide how AI is created, used, and deployed in society. The goal here isn't to stifle innovation but to ensure it's safe, fair, and ethical for everyone. It's like creating a set of guardrails on a rollercoaster ride—keeps the thrills high but the crashes low.

1. The Importance of Ethical AI Development

When we talk about ethics in AI, we're diving into some deep, thought-provoking territory. At the heart of the conversation is this fundamental question: How do we ensure AI aligns with human values? Because let's face it, no one wants a chatbot that insults you when you ask it for help or an algorithm that decides you're not worthy of a loan based on biased data. We can't just allow AI to make decisions in a vacuum. It has to be developed, tested, and monitored with a commitment to fairness, transparency, and respect for human dignity.

This is where AI ethics come into play. We're talking about things like bias mitigation, accountability, and ensuring that AI systems are transparent enough so that the people who use them (and are affected by them) can understand how decisions are being made. Without such frameworks, AI could perpetuate and even exacerbate the inequalities that already exist in society. Think about it—if AI is trained on data that's biased (say, historical data that's discriminatory), then it might make biased decisions. AI doesn't have inherent morality—it's only as good (or bad) as the data and algorithms we feed it. So, yes, ethics in AI is crucial.

2. Creating Clear Regulations for Generative AI

Now, onto regulation—the "buzzkill" part of the AI equation. But hear me out: it's the unsung hero of the AI world. Without regulation, we risk AI models being used in ways that harm society, like creating harmful misinformation, deepfakes, or worse. And with the capabilities of generative AI to create increasingly realistic content, the potential for abuse is high. We've already seen how AI-generated content can be used to manipulate people or spread fake news, so setting boundaries is necessary.

Regulation is needed to establish clear guidelines on how AI should be developed, deployed, and monitored. It's about making sure AI doesn't go rogue or inadvertently harm vulnerable groups. Imagine a world where AI is used responsibly: there would be clear protocols for training AI models, transparent audits, and a strong framework to tackle misuse. Governments, companies, and organizations would work together to ensure that AI benefits society, rather than running unchecked like a freight train.

One example of such regulation can be found in the European Union's Artificial Intelligence Act, which aims to establish clear rules for high-risk AI systems. This act classifies AI into different risk categories, requiring stricter regulations for high-risk uses, such as those in healthcare or criminal justice. By establishing this framework, Europe is trying to balance innovation with safety, and that's exactly what we need on a global scale.

3. AI Accountability and Transparency

Now, let's talk about accountability and transparency, which is the stuff that makes tech giants squirm in their seats. It's one thing to have powerful AI models, but it's quite another to understand how they work. How do we hold AI accountable for its decisions if we don't even know how it made them? This is where transparency and explainability come in.

For example, consider a situation where an AI system wrongly predicts that a job candidate is not a good fit based on biased data. If the candidate doesn't know why they were rejected, how can they challenge the decision? That's where the need for transparent algorithms comes in. We need to make sure that AI systems provide an explanation for their decisions, and that these explanations are accessible to the people affected by them. It's about empowering individuals to understand and potentially contest AI decisions.

Accountability also means that when AI makes a mistake, we can trace it back to the responsible parties—whether that's the developers, the company deploying the system, or both. By having accountability mechanisms in place, we can avoid situations where AI mistakes go unchecked, and the consequences are not felt until it's too late.

4. Balancing Innovation and Regulation

We often hear the term "innovation vs. regulation", and yes, it can seem like a tug of war. On one side, we have innovators, pushing the boundaries of what's possible with generative AI. On the other, we have regulators, attempting to prevent unforeseen consequences and ensure fairness and safety. While it might seem like these two forces are at odds, they actually need each other to create a balanced, thriving AI ecosystem.

The goal is to foster innovation without sacrificing safety. Too much regulation, and you risk stifling creativity and progress. Too little regulation, and you risk opening the door to harmful or unethical practices. It's a fine line, but it's one that's necessary for AI to be a force for good. As the AI industry continues to grow and evolve, we need collaboration between developers, ethicists, regulators, and users to ensure we're headed in the right direction.

5. The Global Nature of AI Regulation

Since AI is global, any regulation we create must be international in scope. AI doesn't know borders—an AI model developed in one country could easily be deployed in another. This creates a challenge for regulators, who must collaborate across nations to ensure consistent standards and ethical practices. The United Nations or other global organizations could play a key role in fostering these international agreements, ensuring that AI benefits everyone, not just those in tech-savvy nations.

A good example of this global approach is the OECD (Organisation for Economic Co-operation and Development), which has worked on AI principles that are intended to guide the ethical development of AI worldwide. It's going to take a lot of effort, but global cooperation on AI regulation will be key to ensuring we avoid a Wild West scenario where some countries are bound by strict regulations, while others operate with minimal oversight.

Conclusion: The Road Ahead

In conclusion, regulation and ethics are not just nice-to-haves—they are absolutely critical for ensuring that generative AI is developed and used in a way that benefits society as a whole. We need clear, actionable regulations to mitigate risks, ensure accountability, and promote ethical behavior in AI development. But we also need innovative thinking and collaboration to strike the right balance between pushing the envelope and safeguarding against harm.

The future of AI is bright, but only if we walk this tightrope carefully. So, let's work together to build an AI-powered world that's not just smarter, but also fairer and more ethical. Because, at the end of the day, we are the ones who shape this future. Let's make it a good one.

10.4 Careers in Generative AI

Ah, careers in Generative AI—just the mention of it probably makes you think of sci-fi movies where AI is in control, maybe even taking over the world (don't worry, we'll leave that plot twist for the next season of your favorite thriller). But in reality, Generative AI has created a wave of exciting, dynamic career opportunities that are transforming industries left, right, and center. This is your chance to hop on the AI train before it reaches its peak. And, trust me, you want to be on board for this one.

So, you might be wondering, "What kind of jobs exist in this mysterious world of Generative AI, and how do I become a part of it?" Great question, my future AI guru! Let's break it down.

1. The AI Engineer: The Architect of the Future

Let's start with the obvious—AI Engineers. These are the folks who design, build, and implement AI systems that can generate text, images, audio, and even video. If you're the type of person who loves working with algorithms, models, and big data, this could be your dream job. AI engineers typically work in machine learning, deep learning, and reinforcement learning, using tools like TensorFlow, PyTorch, or Keras to develop generative models such as GANs, VAEs, and Transformers. In this role, you'll spend your days fine-tuning models, solving complex problems, and contributing to the creation of AI that can mimic human creativity.

It's a high-demand job, especially with the increasing need for advanced generative models in industries like media, gaming, healthcare, and finance. Not only do you need solid programming skills in Python, but understanding the nuances of neural networks, model evaluation, and data processing is a must. If you love the idea of creating systems that think for themselves (in the most ethical way, of course), this career path is an exhilarating ride.

2. The Data Scientist: The Master of Data Alchemy

If you've always seen yourself as the wizard of data, the Data Scientist role is calling your name. In the context of Generative AI, data scientists are crucial for training models. After all, AI isn't magical—it's data-driven! As a data scientist, you'll be responsible for sourcing, cleaning, and manipulating massive datasets that AI models will use to learn and generate output. Your work will help ensure that the AI systems are trained on accurate, representative, and unbiased data, which is an essential part of creating fair AI systems.

Beyond data wrangling, data scientists also work closely with AI engineers to fine-tune models and use statistical methods to understand how well the model performs. It's a highly interdisciplinary role that requires a deep understanding of statistics, machine learning algorithms, and data visualization tools. So, if you've got a passion for working with data and can't resist the challenge of turning raw numbers into meaningful insights, this could be the perfect career for you.

3. The AI Researcher: The Innovator

Now, if you're more of a theoretical thinker who loves to push boundaries and ask, "What if?" then you might want to consider becoming an AI Researcher. These professionals dive into the deeper aspects of artificial intelligence, coming up with new models, algorithms, and methods that push the field forward. AI researchers often work in academia or research labs at companies like Google, OpenAI, and Microsoft, or even start-ups dedicated to cutting-edge AI development.

Their primary role is to advance the theoretical foundations of AI and develop novel architectures. For instance, they could be working on improving existing generative models or proposing new models that help AI systems generate even more sophisticated content. The research could span across multiple domains such as natural language processing, computer vision, or robotics. If you've got a PhD (or are on your way to one), a deep understanding of math and algorithms, and a burning desire to answer big questions about the future of AI, this could be the career for you.

4. The AI Ethics Specialist: The Moral Compass

Here's where things get really interesting—AI Ethics. As Generative AI grows, so does the responsibility of ensuring that these systems are used ethically and responsibly. AI can create powerful content, but if we don't put the proper ethical guidelines in place, it can cause harm, spread misinformation, or perpetuate bias. This is where the AI Ethics Specialist comes in.

In this role, you'll work to ensure that AI systems are designed and deployed in ways that are fair, transparent, and accountable. You'll be the person advocating for the ethical use of AI—creating frameworks and guidelines that minimize harm and promote positive societal impact. You might work alongside AI developers to spot potential biases in datasets, help design systems that are explainable to users, or ensure that AI-generated content is used responsibly. If you're passionate about ensuring that technology doesn't run wild and love balancing innovation with moral considerations, this is an area ripe for exploration.

5. The AI Product Manager: The Bridge Between Creativity and Technology

If you've ever found yourself in a room full of developers and thought, "I can make this work," then a Product Manager role in AI might be right up your alley. As an AI Product Manager, you'll be the link between the technical team and the business side, helping translate customer needs into AI-driven solutions. You'll work closely with engineers, data scientists, and designers to ensure the development of AI products that meet user needs, are feasible, and are aligned with ethical considerations.

The exciting part? You'll be able to see the tangible impact of your work—whether it's AI tools for content creation, personalized recommendations, or automated services—on real-world products. If you love seeing big ideas come to life and you're comfortable juggling both technical and business aspects, AI product management offers one of the most dynamic and rewarding career paths.

6. The AI Entrepreneur: The Visionary Innovator

Of course, if you've ever thought about starting your own AI company, then this is your call to action. As a Generative AI entrepreneur, you could be the next visionary creating the next big thing in AI—from generative tools to content creation platforms or even tools that revolutionize industries like healthcare, education, or entertainment. With the AI space being as dynamic and fast-moving as it is, the opportunities are endless for those with a combination of tech-savvy, business acumen, and the ability to spot gaps in the market.

This role requires a unique set of skills that blend technology, business strategy, and a vision for the future. You'll need a strong understanding of AI, but you'll also need to know how to scale a business, build a team, and bring an idea to life. If you've got the drive to launch the next great AI-driven product and lead a team of innovators, entrepreneurship in the world of Generative AI might be your perfect playground.

7. The AI Instructor/Trainer: The Mentor of the Future

Lastly, as AI becomes increasingly prevalent, the demand for people who can teach and train others on AI principles will soar. This is where AI instructors and trainers come in. If you love helping others understand complex concepts and want to be at the forefront of educating the next generation of AI professionals, this could be your calling.

Whether you're teaching AI theory in a university or providing hands-on training through workshops and courses, educating the workforce on AI will be a critical role as the industry continues to grow. By sharing your knowledge and helping others navigate the exciting (and sometimes intimidating) world of AI, you'll have a front-row seat to the evolution of the industry.

Conclusion: Embrace Your Future in Generative AI

The field of Generative AI is expanding rapidly, and with that growth comes a plethora of career opportunities. Whether you're inclined to the technical side, the creative side, or the ethical side, there's a place for you in this revolution. Generative AI is transforming industries, and the skills you'll develop in this space will be highly sought after in the coming years.

So, if you're intrigued by the endless possibilities of AI-powered creativity, and you're ready to take your career to the next level, now's the time to dive in. Your future in Generative AI is waiting—just make sure you bring your curiosity, creativity, and sense of adventure along for the ride!

10.5 How to Keep Learning and Stay Current

Ah, the world of Generative AI—it's like a party that never ends! And like any good party, things are always changing: new technologies pop up, new models are developed, and just when you think you've learned it all, BAM, another breakthrough happens. It's like trying to keep up with the latest trends in fashion—except, instead of wearing neon green pants, you're integrating the newest neural networks into your models. But don't worry, I've got you covered with some strategies on how to keep learning and stay current in the fast-moving world of AI.

First things first: don't think of learning as a destination. It's a journey, my friend—like trying to conquer an epic video game. You level up, but then a new expansion pack comes out, and suddenly you're back to square one. The key here is to embrace the chaos.

Generative AI isn't about knowing everything in one go (spoiler alert: no one does). Instead, it's about staying curious, staying humble, and most importantly, staying engaged with the ever-evolving landscape. It's all about lifelong learning—just without the fancy cap and gown (unless you really want one, in which case, go for it).

1. Stay Engaged with the AI Community

You're not in this alone. Join the AI community—whether it's through forums, discussion groups, or meetups. Sites like Reddit, Stack Overflow, and GitHub are buzzing with AI enthusiasts from around the globe. You'll find cutting-edge research, tutorials, code snippets, and a constant flow of new ideas that will help you stay on the pulse of the latest trends. The AI community is like a global think tank—people sharing knowledge, solving problems, and pushing the boundaries of what's possible.

In addition to online spaces, consider attending AI-related events, such as conferences or webinars. NeurIPS, ICML, and CVPR are some of the heavyweights in AI conferences. These events are packed with brilliant minds, the latest research, and potential collaborators. Plus, if you like feeling like a rock star surrounded by other rock stars, these events are perfect. Networking at these events can be just as valuable as the content itself, helping you stay connected with leaders in the field.

2. Online Courses and Tutorials

Let's be real: sometimes, books are awesome (I mean, I wrote one, after all), but when it comes to hands-on AI, nothing beats a good online course. And I'm talking about the latest, trendiest courses out there. Think about it: if a new Generative AI framework drops, you want to be on top of it right away, not months later. Platforms like Coursera, Udemy, and edX are great for keeping your skills fresh. They often offer free courses or affordable subscriptions, and best of all, they let you learn at your own pace. That means no stressing over a 9 a.m. lecture (unless you really enjoy that, then by all means, power to you).

Also, don't overlook platforms like Kaggle, where you can dive deep into datasets and participate in competitions that challenge your AI skills. Kaggle competitions aren't just about winning prizes (although that's fun too), they're a great way to learn by applying what you know and tackling real-world problems.

3. Research Papers and Preprints

You've probably heard this a thousand times, but it's worth repeating: if you want to be on the cutting edge of AI, you've got to be reading the research. ArXiv and Google Scholar are your best friends here. These platforms host a constant stream of research papers on the latest developments in AI, including groundbreaking papers on Generative AI. By reading papers, you get insight into the theories, methods, and algorithms that are shaping the future of AI, often before they make it to a textbook or blog post.

While reading academic papers can be intimidating at first (seriously, they sound like they're written in another language), it gets easier with time. And don't feel bad if you don't understand everything on your first pass—that's part of the process! Start with survey papers (which give you an overview of a field) and work your way into more specific topics. Before long, you'll be citing papers in your own work.

4. Experiment, Build, Break, Repeat

You want to learn AI? Well, the best way is to get your hands dirty. It's one thing to read about Generative AI, but it's another thing entirely to actually build models and create your own generative projects. Want to know the real secret to keeping up with the field? It's experimenting. Build text generation models, create image synthesis systems, or even dive into music composition with AI. The more you build, the more you learn.

Even when things go wrong (and trust me, they will—it's like AI's version of a rite of passage), that's when you learn the most. Troubleshooting bugs and finding creative solutions to problems is how you sharpen your skills. So go ahead and mess around with a new tool, library, or framework, and don't be afraid to fail. In fact, celebrate the failures—because they're learning opportunities wrapped in code.

5. Follow Industry News and Blogs

The world of Generative AI is always changing, and keeping track of the latest developments is crucial. Luckily, the AI media ecosystem is thriving, with news websites, blogs, and newsletters dedicated to AI breakthroughs. Websites like The AI Report, TechCrunch, and VentureBeat regularly publish updates on the newest trends, acquisitions, and innovations in the AI world.

Also, don't forget about AI blogs! Experts in the field, like those at OpenAI, DeepMind, and Fast.ai, frequently post updates on the latest research, tutorials, and insights. Subscribing to these blogs and newsletters means that you'll always have the most recent information delivered straight to your inbox, giving you the competitive edge when it comes to staying current.

6. Collaborate and Contribute to Open Source

AI is a collaborative field, and there's no better way to stay current than by working with others. Collaborating on projects, contributing to open-source AI initiatives, or even just discussing ideas with peers is essential for continued growth. GitHub is the prime platform for collaboration, with countless open-source AI projects where you can contribute code, submit bug fixes, or even launch your own projects.

By working on these projects, you'll not only keep up with the field, but you'll also develop valuable networking connections and gain exposure to new ideas, libraries, and techniques that you might not have encountered on your own.

Conclusion: Embrace the Journey

In conclusion, staying current in Generative AI is like riding a roller coaster—it's fast, it's thrilling, and it keeps you on your toes. But just like any roller coaster, it's worth the ride. By staying engaged with the community, constantly learning, and experimenting with new tools and techniques, you'll always be ready to face the next big breakthrough. So keep your curiosity alive, your mind open, and never stop learning. After all, AI is a journey, not a destination—so buckle up and enjoy the ride!

Now go ahead and stay ahead of the curve. The future of Generative AI is waiting for you, and it's looking brighter (and smarter) than ever.

Well, look at you. You made it. From your first curious peek into the world of artificial intelligence to casually tossing around terms like "latent space" and "diffusion model" like a seasoned tech sorcerer. If you're feeling a little smarter, slightly more powerful, and maybe even dangerously inspired to build something epic—good. That was the plan.

We've gone on quite a ride in this book—from defining AI in all its sci-fi-meets-reality glory, to exploring how machines are now creating text, images, music, and memes that rival human creativity (or at least confuse the internet). You've learned the basics of machine learning, built your first generative projects, peeked under the hood of powerful models like GANs and Transformers, and even touched on the deep philosophical questions: "What does it mean if a robot writes poetry?" and "Should I let it?"

And while this might be the final chapter of this book, it's nowhere near the end of your journey. This is just Book One in *The Generative AI Blueprint, a series* I wrote because—honestly—I couldn't shut up about AI. If this book was your friendly intro, the rest of the series is where we really roll up our sleeves and build some wild stuff together.

You ready to level up? Here's what's coming next:

Python for AI: Build Generative Models from Scratch – Let's get you coding like a pro.

Deep Learning Essentials: Master Neural Networks for AI – Time to sculpt those digital brains.

Autoencoders & VAEs: Hands-On Generative AI Projects – For when you want to start creating weirdly impressive things.

GANs in Action: Create Realistic Images & Videos with AI – The AI artist in you will love this one.

Transformers & GPT: Build and Fine-Tune Large Language Models – Because the world needs more chatbot philosophers.

Stable Diffusion & AI Art: Generate Stunning Images with AI – Seriously, this one is just visual candy.

Multimodal AI: How to Combine Text, Images & Video with AI – Where things start to feel truly futuristic.

Fine-Tuning & Deploying AI Models: A Practical Guide – So your creations don't just live on your laptop.

The Future of Generative AI: Ethics, Careers & Business Applications – Real talk about where this is all going and what role you can play.

But before you charge ahead, I want to say thank you. Sincerely. Writing this book was a mix of excitement, obsession, and more than a few late-night debugging sessions. But knowing it landed in your hands—and hopefully sparked a few "Whoa, this is awesome!" moments—makes every bit of it worth it.

So whether you're a student, a hobbyist, an artist, or just someone who wants to understand the tech that's reshaping our world, I'm glad we crossed paths. Keep exploring, keep experimenting, and don't be afraid to build something that makes people go, "Wait... a robot made that?"

You've got this.

See you in the next book.

—*Aeronis Krynn*

www.ingramcontent.com/pod-product-compliance
Lightning Source LLC
LaVergne TN
LVHW060121070326
832902LV00019B/3079